25 YEARS *of* FAVORITE BRAND NAME RECIPES™

Publications International, Ltd.

Favorite Brand Name Recipes at www.fbnr.com

Pictured on the front cover *(top row, left to right):* Toll House® Mini Morsel Pancakes *(page 12),* Rapid Ragú® Chili *(page 138)* and Stuffed Portobello Mushrooms *(page 80); (second row, left to right)* Ortega® Green Chile Guacamole *(page 232),* Simple Stir-Fry *(page 126)* and Nestlé® Toll House® Chocolate Chip Pie *(page 326); (third row, left to right)* Harvest Pot Roast *(page 172),* Blackened Catfish with Creole Vegetables *(page 204)* and Pumpkin Spiced and Iced Cookies *(page 358).*

Pictured on the back cover *(clockwise from top):* Mexican Pepper Steak *(page 150),* Field Green Salad with Balsamic Vinaigrette *(page 62)* and Peanut Butter Fudge Brownie Bars *(page 360).*

ISBN-13: 978-1-4127-2492-0
ISBN-10: 1-4127-2492-9

Library of Congress Control Number: 2006903675

Manufactured in China.

8 7 6 5 4 3 2 1

Microwave Cooking: Microwave ovens vary in wattage. Use the cooking times as guidelines and check for doneness before adding more time.

Preparation/Cooking Times: Preparation times are based on the approximate amount of time required to assemble the recipe before cooking, baking, chilling or serving. These times include preparation steps such as measuring, chopping and mixing. The fact that some preparations and cooking can be done simultaneously is taken into account. Preparation of optional ingredients and serving suggestions is not included.

Contents

25 Years of All-American Favorites from Brands You Trust

Good recipes are like good friends—you can always depend on them. Chances are you already have a recipe box filled with well-used, food-stained index cards. If some of your favorites came from the back of a box or the label on a jar, then this cookbook is for you.

You'll find the very best recipes developed over the last 25 years in test kitchens across the country. Some may be familiar, like Original Green Bean Casserole. Others will be a delightful surprise. (How about Cavemen Beef Back Ribs?) Every recipe has been tested extensively by home economists at the food companies and associations whose products are featured. You can be sure these recipes will not only work, they'll wow you every time. After all, who knows better how to get the best out of their brands than the companies who make them?

Because this book was written with the home cook in mind, dishes are designed for families, not fancy restaurants. Although some of the fabulous desserts included here would put many restaurants to shame! There are no hard-to-find exotic ingredients in these recipes, no expensive equipment to buy, no tricky techniques to master. In fact, you can pull together many of the dishes from ingredients already in your pantry.

From cookies to casseroles, tacos to tuna casserole, this book is a celebration of America's unique way with food. No place else on earth offers such a diverse array of flavors and choices. For a delicious trip down memory lane, check out some of the highs (and lows) of American home cooking in the last century on the following pages. Then get ready to make some food memories of your own with the recipes in the pages of *25 Years of Favorite Brand Name Recipes*™.

A Century of American Home Cooking

1900–1920

Fanny Farmer Measured Up

Fannie Merritt Farmer started a revolution in home cooking with *The Boston Cooking-School Cook Book.* Farmer's book used level measures and precise amounts instead of the vague quantities given in most recipes of the time, which specified ingredients by the "teacup full" if they even bothered with amounts.

A Cartoonist Turned Franks into Hot Dogs

The St. Louis World's Fair in 1904 introduced burgers on buns, ice cream cones, popcorn and iced tea among other wonders. Frankfurters became hot dogs after a cartoonist drew a dachshund on a bun. Tuna in cans, tea in bags, marshmallow fluff and machine-made peanut butter made their appearance.

Lady Baltimore and Oysters Rockefeller Ruled

The optimism of the new century brought a taste for indulgence—Lady Baltimore Cake, Oysters Rockefeller and Vichyssoise were popular. Fortunately being plump was in fashion. President Taft, whose favorite meal was Lobster Thermidor, weighed in at 300 pounds.

More Americans Were Cooking with Gas

At home, gas ranges began to phase out wood-fired stoves. An even more revolutionary change was taking place outside the home—the introduction of self-service grocery stores.

Gelatin Wiggled Its Way into the Pantry

Packaged gelatin was a solid success with home cooks. Prior to its introduction the only way to make a "congealed" salad was to boil calves feet—a time consuming, labor intensive project. In 1905 a Pennsylvania woman won a contest with her recipe for "Perfection Salad." It featured bits of celery, cabbage and bell pepper suspended in gelatin, and instantly became an American classic.

A 1900's Menu

Oysters Rockefeller

Vichyssoise

"Congealed" (gelatin) Salad

Lobster Thermidor and/or Roast Elk

Lady Baltimore Cake

1920–1940

Marshmallows, Pineapple and All That Jazz

The Jazz Age celebrated the convenience of pineapples in cans from Hawaii, and marshmallows made in a factory by putting these two ingredients in everything from salad to frosting. Some of these recipes, like Heavenly Hash and Pineapple Upside Down Cake, we still enjoy today.

The Big Chill Was On

In the United States refrigerator sales topped 800,000 units. The average price—$292. (By 1939 it went down to $169.) Powered by electricity, the new refrigerators were a huge improvement on the old icebox, which was unreliable, hard to clean and had to be constantly supplied with blocks of ice.

The Best Thing Since Sliced Bread

It stayed fresh, came in a convenient reclosable wrap and, best of all, was perfectly sliced. The 1920's were the beginning of the American love affair with white bread. By 1923 you could buy it at any of the 14,000 A & P grocery stores nationwide.

Betty Crocker Was "Born"

An adman's invention in 1921, the spokesperson for Gold Medal flour was given the name Betty because it sounded friendly. It was her radio show "Betty Crocker Cooking School of the Air" several years later that started her transformation into trusted household cooking authority. Folks were so convinced she was real, they frequently sent her letters and even gifts. Betty has since undergone six major makeovers to keep up with changing styles.

Frosted Food Heated Up

It was an accident that gave Clarence Birdseye the idea for frozen foods. While fishing in Labrador he discovered that the icy waters froze fish rock hard and also preserved its freshness and flavor. In 1929 Birds Eye® Frosted Foods was launched. It was an idea whose time had come. Even though frozen foods cost more and despite the fact that the country was in the Great Depression, Birds Eye® Frosted Foods were an immediate and long-term success.

1940–1960

The Home Front Battled Wartime Shortages

Meat, sugar, butter, milk, eggs and coffee were rationed during World War II. Clever homemakers cheerfully invented hundreds of new recipes to cope with the shortages. Recipes for eggless, milkless, butterless cakes and mock apple pies appeared in magazines. Tips on stretching meat included some questionable ideas (mock duck made of red lentils) and some recipes we still enjoy today (meat loaf).

Babies, Barbecues and Beef Stroganoff Boomed

The postwar economy boomed. There were more babies, more jobs, more homes being built, more time and more money. Suburban living was celebrated with the backyard barbecue. This manly endeavor usually involved large slabs of meat, then in plentiful supply. Inside, in ultraclean, ultramodern kitchens, homemakers created gourmet dishes from convenience foods. Beef Stroganoff made with canned mushroom soup was perfect for elegant entertaining, especially when served from a chafing dish.

The Perfect Dip with the Perfect Martini

New York City sold out of clams within 24 hours when the first recipe for clam dip appeared on a TV commercial. At the fifties cocktail party canapés were deemed old fashioned, but dips were divine. The martini had been around since before the turn of the century, but in the fifties making the perfect dry martini became the source of endless discussion and raucous experimentation.

Dining Tables Turned into TV Trays

Television sets became more affordable and there were more and more programs to watch. In 1953 the first TV dinner was introduced in a package designed to look like a TV screen. For a mere 98 cents, there was turkey, stuffing, gravy, whipped sweet potatoes and peas all snuggled into separate compartments in an aluminum tray. TV dinners were welcomed as the ultimate time- and energy-saver. There weren't even any dishes to wash!

Crazy for Cake

Between 1947 and 1948 General Mills and Pillsbury both introduced cake mixes, but the real cake craze of the forties was chiffon cake. Hailed as the first new cake in a hundred years, chiffon cake was made with salad oil instead of butter or shortening. Recipes offered dozens of flavors from lemon to peppermint chip.

1960–1980

Julia Taught Us French

More and more cooks were embracing the idea of "gourmet" food, but most of them were doing it with one hand on a can opener. That is, until Julia Child came along to prove that French cooking could be accessible and authentic. Her thorough recipes and delightfully eccentric manner charmed the country. Cooking schools and equipment stores spread rapidly with her popularity.

Exotic Food Became Mainstream

Pupu platters and mai tais served amid frowning tiki gods made restaurants like Trader Vic's a huge success. Polynesian-themed parties, complete with umbrellas in the drinks, were also considered a sophisticated way to entertain at home. This yen for the exotic extended to tropical fruit. The kiwi (originally named Chinese gooseberry) appeared in markets in the early seventies. Before long the trendy kiwi showed up in desserts, salads, salsas and more.

Microwaves Made Waves

The first microwave oven was nearly six feet tall and weighed 700 pounds. By 1976, however, microwaves had been slimmed down to counter-top size and made affordable; almost 60 percent of households had one. The microwave had become an indispensable part of fast-paced American life.

Gourmet a Go-Go

Convenience foods were not only time-savers, they were considered sophisticated, hip, and in the language of the day—a go-go. They were freely used to invent some pretty unusual "gourmet" concoctions. Crème Mongole was canned pea soup mixed with cream of tomato. For a fancy "en croute" entrée, almost any food could be (and was) wrapped in packaged piecrust. Mercifully, most of these stunning examples of "a go-go" are long gone.

Crock-Pots® and Cuisinarts® Crowded Countertops.

Cooks have always loved gadgets, and by the late seventies blenders were not enough. Food processors, introduced at the 1973 housewares show, were newer and sexier. Even better was the slow cooker, a rather homely-looking appliance that was a beautiful way to cook dinner while you were away at work, which more and more women were.

1980–2000

Pizza with Everything

America's first pizzeria opened in 1905, but it was in the eighties that pizza moved beyond its Italian roots to become gourmet. It came topped with goat cheese, grilled vegetables and even barbecued chicken.

Health Food Became Healthful Food

Health food as in wheat germ and carrot juice had been around for a while, but it took the eighties to make healthful eating a national obsession. Celebrity chefs boasted about using organic produce and free-range chickens. Spa cuisine (in which you pay big bucks for small portions) was born. Red meat was something to be feared and oat bran was all the rage.

Americans Learned to Salsa

In the nineties salsa sales surpassed ketchup sales. Mexican, Tex-Mex, Santa Fe and Southwestern cuisines were hotter than the desert in the afternoon. Spicy was good and eating the hottest chiles you could handle practically became a national sport.

Comfort Food Made a Comeback

Tired of elaborately stacked food and fancy squiggles of sauce, Americans yearned for simpler pleasures, like mashed potatoes and meat loaf. Diner food became chic and humble dishes got gussied up. What could be more representative of America's melting pot culture than macaroni and cheese made with cavatappi pasta and shiitake mushrooms?

What's Next?

Ethnic food is hot (with or without the chile peppers) and getting hotter. Health-conscious cooks are checking labels and demanding more nutrition for their shopping dollars. Cooking classes are offered everywhere from the mall to the market. Chefs are now pop stars. Americans are more interested than ever in food, and yet have less time to cook! While nobody knows for sure what the future holds, you can bet your fondue pot it will be a delicious surprise.

A 1980's Menu

Mesclun Salad with Goat Cheese

Pizza with Roasted Peppers and Garlic

Blackened Redfish with Fresh Salsa

Sauteéd Baby Vegetables

Tiramisu

Breakfast & Brunch

Days seem to start out right when they include a great breakfast. From a Bacon, Avocado and Cheese Omelet to Ortega® Huevos Rancheros, you'll find a recipe here to suit your morning style whether you're an early riser or prefer sleeping until noon. Give the kids a treat and whip up some Toll House® Mini Morsel Pancakes. Have friends over for brunch and delight them with Stuffed French Toast with Fresh Berry Topping. One taste of any of these delicious dishes is guaranteed to turn even the grumpiest sleepyhead into a morning person.

Toll House® Mini Morsel Pancakes

  2½ cups all-purpose flour
    1 cup (6 ounces) NESTLÉ® TOLL HOUSE® Semi-Sweet Chocolate Mini Morsels
    1 tablespoon baking powder
    ½ teaspoon salt
  1¾ cups milk
    2 eggs
    ⅓ cup vegetable oil
    ⅓ cup packed brown sugar
      Powdered sugar
      Fresh sliced strawberries
      Maple syrup

COMBINE flour, morsels, baking powder and salt in large bowl. Combine milk, eggs, vegetable oil and brown sugar in medium bowl; add to flour mixture. Stir just until moistened (batter may be lumpy).

HEAT griddle or skillet over medium heat; brush lightly with vegetable oil. Pour ¼ *cup* of batter onto hot griddle; cook until bubbles begin to burst. Turn; continue to cook for about 1 minute longer or until golden. Repeat with *remaining* batter.

SPRINKLE with powdered sugar; top with strawberries. Serve with maple syrup.

Makes about 18 pancakes

Honey Custard French Toast

    ½ cup honey
    1 cup milk
    6 eggs
  1½ teaspoons cinnamon
    ⅛ teaspoon salt
  12 slices (¾-inch thick) French bread
      Butter
      Honey and toasted pecan pieces

In large bowl, beat together honey, milk, eggs, cinnamon and salt. Dip bread slices in egg mixture, turning to coat. Brown soaked slices in butter over medium heat, turning once. Serve with honey and sprinkle with pecans, if desired.

Makes 6 servings

*Favorite recipe from **National Honey Board***

Bacon, Avocado and Cheese Omelet

Salsa

> 2 cups finely chopped seeded tomato
> ½ cup finely chopped onion
> 2 jalapeño peppers*, or to taste, seeded and minced
> 4 tablespoons minced fresh cilantro
> 3 tablespoons fresh lime or lemon juice
>   Salt and black pepper

Omelet

> 12 large eggs
> 6 tablespoons water
>   Salt and black pepper to taste
> 3 tablespoons CRISCO® Shortening or 3 tablespoons CRISCO® Stick, divided
> 9 slices lean bacon, cooked and crumbled
> 2 small avocados, peeled and cut into ½-inch pieces
> 1½ cups coarsely grated Monterey Jack cheese

Jalapeño peppers can sting and irritate the skin; wear rubber gloves when handling peppers and do not touch your eyes.

Salsa

Stir together, in a small bowl, tomato, onion, jalapeños, cilantro, lime juice, and salt and pepper to taste.

Omelets

Whisk together the eggs, water, salt and pepper in a medium bowl.

Heat ½ tablespoon CRISCO Shortening in an 8-inch skillet, preferably non-stick, over moderately-high heat, until the foam subsides.

Pour ⅙ egg mixture evenly over bottom of skillet. Cook for 1 minute or until it is set.

Sprinkle ½ the omelet with ⅙ of the bacon, ⅙ of the avocado and ⅙ of the Monterey Jack cheese; cook the omelet for 1 minute or until set.

Fold the omelet over the filling, transfer to a plate and keep warm.

Repeat in the same manner with the remaining CRISCO, egg mixture, bacon, avocado and Monterey Jack cheese.

Serve omelets with salsa.

Makes 6 servings

Bacon, Avocado and Cheese Omelet

Orange Streusel Coffeecake

    Cocoa Streusel (recipe follows)
¾ **cup (1½ sticks) butter or margarine, softened**
 1 **cup sugar**
 3 **eggs**
 1 **teaspoon vanilla extract**
½ **cup dairy sour cream**
 3 **cups all-purpose flour**
 2 **teaspoons baking powder**
 1 **teaspoon baking soda**
 1 **cup orange juice**
 2 **teaspoons grated orange peel**
½ **cup orange marmalade or apple jelly**

1. Prepare Cocoa Streusel. Heat oven to 350°F. Generously grease 12-cup fluted tube pan.

2. Beat butter and sugar in large bowl until well blended. Add eggs and vanilla; beat well. Add sour cream; beat until blended. Stir together flour, baking powder and baking soda; add alternately with orange juice to butter mixture, beating until well blended. Stir in orange peel.

3. Spread marmalade in bottom of prepared pan; sprinkle half of streusel over marmalade. Pour half of batter into pan, spreading evenly. Sprinkle remaining streusel over batter; spread remaining batter evenly over streusel.

4. Bake about 1 hour or until toothpick inserted near center of cake comes out clean. Loosen cake from side of pan with metal spatula; immediately invert onto serving plate. Serve warm or cool. *Makes 12 servings*

Cocoa Streusel: Stir together ⅔ cup packed light brown sugar, ½ cup chopped walnuts, ¼ cup HERSHEY'S Cocoa and ½ cup MOUNDS® Sweetened Coconut Flakes, if desired.

Orange Streusel Coffeecake

Country Skillet Hash

2 tablespoons butter or margarine
4 boneless pork chops (¾ inch thick), diced
¼ teaspoon black pepper
¼ teaspoon cayenne pepper (optional)
1 medium onion, chopped
2 cloves garlic, minced
1 can (14½ ounces) DEL MONTE® Whole New Potatoes, drained and diced
1 can (14½ ounces) DEL MONTE Stewed Tomatoes - Original Recipe, undrained*
1 medium green bell pepper, chopped
½ teaspoon thyme, crushed

May substitute DEL MONTE Diced Tomatoes, undrained.

1. Melt butter in large skillet over medium heat. Add meat; cook, stirring occasionally, until no longer pink in center. Season with black pepper and cayenne pepper, if desired.

2. Add onion and garlic; cook until tender. Stir in potatoes, tomatoes, green pepper and thyme. Cook 5 minutes, stirring frequently. Season with salt, if desired.   *Makes 4 servings*

Tip: The hash may be topped with a poached or fried egg.

Prep Time: 10 minutes
Cook Time: 15 minutes

Country Skillet Hash

Cheesy Potato Pancakes

1½ **quarts prepared instant mashed potatoes, cooked dry and cooled**
1½ **cups (6 ounces) shredded Wisconsin Colby or Muenster cheese**
  4 **eggs, lightly beaten**
1½ **cups all-purpose flour, divided**
  ¾ **cup chopped fresh parsley**
  ⅓ **cup chopped fresh chives**
1½ **teaspoons dried thyme, rosemary or sage leaves**
  2 **eggs, lightly beaten**

1. In large bowl, combine potatoes, cheese, 4 beaten eggs, ¾ cup flour and herbs; mix well. Cover and refrigerate at least 4 hours before molding and preparing.

2. To prepare, form 18 (3-inch) patties. Dip in 2 beaten eggs and dredge in remaining ¾ cup flour. Cook each patty in nonstick skillet over medium heat 3 minutes per side or until crisp, golden brown and heated through. *Makes 4 to 6 servings*

Serving Suggestion: Serve warm with eggs or omelets, or serve with sour cream and sliced pan-fried apples or applesauce.

Variation: Substitute Wisconsin Cheddar or Smoked Cheddar for Colby or Muenster.

Favorite recipe from **Wisconsin Milk Marketing Board**

Breakfast Kabobs

2 **cups plain yogurt**
4 **tablespoons honey**
1 **(12-ounce) package BOB EVANS® Original or Maple Links**
1 **medium cantaloupe melon, peeled, seeded and cut into 1-inch cubes**
1 **medium honeydew melon, peeled, seeded and cut into 1-inch cubes**
1 **small bunch green seedless grapes**
1 **small bunch red seedless grapes**
2 **medium red apples, cored and cut into 1-inch cubes**
1 **pint strawberries, hulled and cut into halves**

Combine yogurt and honey in small bowl; refrigerate until ready to serve. Cook sausage in medium skillet over medium heat until browned. Drain on paper towels; cut each link in half. Alternately place sausage and fruit on wooden skewers (about 7). Serve kabobs with yogurt sauce for dipping. *Makes about 7 kabobs*

Cheesy Potato Pancakes

Spinach & Egg Casserole

1 box (10 ounces) BIRDS EYE® frozen Chopped Spinach
1 can (15 ounces) Cheddar cheese soup
1 tablespoon mustard
½ pound deli ham, cut into ¼-inch cubes
4 hard-boiled eggs, chopped or sliced

• Preheat oven to 350°F.

• In large saucepan, cook spinach according to package directions; drain well.

• Stir in soup, mustard and ham.

• Pour into 9×9-inch baking pan. Top with eggs.

• Bake 15 to 20 minutes or until heated through.

Makes 4 servings

Serving Suggestion: Sprinkle with paprika for added color.

Birds Eye Idea: Cook eggs the day before and refrigerate. They will be much easier to peel.

Prep Time: 10 minutes
Cook Time: 15 to 20 minutes

Breakfast Waffle Club Sandwich with Honey Apple Syrup

¾ cup honey, divided
¼ cup apple juice
2 tablespoons butter or margarine
2 crisp red apples, cored and sliced
8 frozen waffles, toasted
8 thin slices ham

To prepare syrup, place ½ cup honey and apple juice in small saucepan over medium heat; heat through. Set aside and keep warm. Melt butter with remaining ¼ cup honey in large nonstick skillet over medium-high heat. Add apples; cook and stir about 4 minutes or until apples are lightly caramelized and crisp-tender. For each serving, place 2 waffles on plate, overlapping slightly. Top each waffle with 1 slice ham. Top with ¼ of apple mixture and drizzle with ¼ of syrup.

Makes 4 servings

Favorite recipe from **National Honey Board**

Spinach & Egg Casserole

Cheddar Broccoli Quiche

1½ **cups milk**
3 **eggs**
1 **package KNORR® Recipe Classics™ Leek recipe mix**
1 **package (10 ounces) frozen chopped broccoli, thawed and drained**
1½ **cups shredded Cheddar, Swiss or Monterey Jack cheese (about 6 ounces)**
1 **(9-inch) unbaked or frozen deep-dish pie crust***

*If using 9-inch deep-dish frozen prepared pie crust, do not thaw. Preheat oven and cookie sheet. Pour filling into pie crust; bake on cookie sheet.

• Preheat oven to 375°F. In large bowl, with fork, beat milk, eggs and recipe mix until blended. Stir in broccoli and cheese; spoon into pie crust.

• Bake 40 minutes or until knife inserted 1 inch from edge comes out clean. Let stand 10 minutes before serving. *Makes 6 servings*

Recipe Tip: Cheddar Broccoli Quiche accompanied with fresh fruit or cherry tomatoes is perfect for brunch or lunch. Or serve it with a mixed green salad and soup for a hearty dinner.

Prep Time: 10 minutes
Cook Time: 40 minutes

Fruit-n-Grain Breakfast Salad

3 **cups water**
¼ **teaspoon salt**
¾ **cup uncooked quick-cooking brown rice**
¾ **cup uncooked bulgur**
1 **Washington Granny Smith apple**
1 **Washington Red Delicious apple**
1 **orange**
1 **cup raisins**
8 **ounces low-fat vanilla yogurt**

In large pot, bring water and salt to boil over high heat. Add rice and bulgur; reduce heat to low. Cover and cook 10 minutes. Remove from heat and set aside, covered, for 2 minutes. Spread hot grains on baking sheet to cool. (Grains can be cooked ahead of time and stored in refrigerator up to one week.) Just before serving, prepare fruit. Core and chop apples. Peel orange and cut into sections. Add chopped apple, orange sections and raisins to cooled grain mixture. Add yogurt and stir to coat grains and fruit. *Makes 6 servings*

*Favorite recipe from **Washington Apple Commission***

Cheddar Broccoli Quiche

Egg and Sausage Breakfast Strudel

1 pound BOB EVANS® Original Recipe Roll Sausage
¾ cup finely grated Parmesan cheese
1 (10¾-ounce) can condensed cream of mushroom soup
2 hard-cooked eggs, cut into ¼-inch cubes
½ cup thinly sliced green onions
¼ cup chopped fresh parsley
1 (16-ounce) package frozen phyllo dough, thawed according to package directions
Butter-flavored nonstick cooking spray *or* ½ cup melted butter or margarine

Crumble and cook sausage in medium skillet until browned. Drain off any drippings; place sausage in medium bowl. Add cheese, soup, eggs, green onions and parsley; stir gently until blended. Cover and chill at least 4 hours.

Preheat oven to 375°F. Layer 4 sheets of phyllo dough, coating each sheet with cooking spray or brushing with melted butter before stacking. Cut stack in half lengthwise. Shape ⅓ cup filling into log and place at bottom end of 1 stack. Fold in sides to cover filling; roll up phyllo dough and filling jelly-roll style. Seal edges and spray roll with cooking spray or brush with butter. Repeat with remaining phyllo dough and filling. Place rolls on ungreased baking sheet, seam sides down. Bake 15 to 20 minutes or until golden brown. Serve hot. Refrigerate leftovers.

Makes 10 strudels

Note: Unbaked strudels can be wrapped and refrigerated up to 24 hours, or frozen up to 1 month. If frozen, allow additional baking time.

Country Fare Breakfast with Wisconsin Fontina

¼ **cup (½ stick) butter**
2 **cups frozen hash brown potatoes**
¼ **cup finely chopped onion**
6 **eggs, beaten**
2 **tablespoons milk**
¾ **teaspoon salt**
⅛ **teaspoon pepper**
¼ **cup chopped fresh parsley, divided**
1 **cup (4 ounces) shredded Wisconsin Fontina cheese, divided**
1 **cup cubed cooked turkey**

Melt butter in 10-inch ovenproof skillet; add potatoes and onion. Cook, covered, over medium heat 15 minutes until tender and lightly browned; stir occasionally. Beat together eggs, milk, salt and pepper; stir in 3 tablespoons parsley and ½ cup cheese. Pour egg mixture over potatoes; sprinkle with turkey. Bake, uncovered, in preheated 350°F oven for 20 minutes or until eggs are set. Sprinkle remaining ½ cup cheese over eggs; return to oven for about 2 minutes until cheese is melted. Remove from oven and garnish with remaining parsley. Cut into wedges and serve with salsa, if desired. *Makes 6 servings*

Note: Ham can be substituted for turkey.

Favorite recipe from **Wisconsin Milk Marketing Board**

Stuffed French Toast with Fresh Berry Topping

2 cups mixed fresh berries (strawberries, raspberries, blueberries and/or blackberries)
2 tablespoons granulated sugar
⅔ cup low-fat ricotta cheese
¼ cup strawberry preserves
3 large eggs
⅔ cup (5-fluid-ounce can) NESTLÉ® CARNATION® Evaporated Fat Free Milk
2 tablespoons packed brown sugar
2 teaspoons vanilla extract
12 slices (about ¾-inch-thick) French bread
1 tablespoon vegetable oil, butter or margarine
Powdered sugar (optional)
Maple syrup, heated (optional)

COMBINE berries and granulated sugar in small bowl. Combine ricotta cheese and strawberry preserves in another small bowl; mix well. Combine eggs, evaporated milk, brown sugar and vanilla extract in pie plate or shallow bowl; mix well.

SPREAD ricotta-preserve mixture evenly over *6 slices* of bread. Top with *remaining* slices of bread to form sandwiches.

HEAT vegetable oil or butter in large, nonstick skillet or griddle over medium heat. Dip sandwiches in egg mixture, coating both sides. Cook on each side for about 2 minutes or until golden brown.

SPRINKLE with powdered sugar; top with berries. Serve with maple syrup, if desired

Makes 6 servings

Stuffed French Toast with Fresh Berry Topping

Ortega® Huevos Rancheros

2 tablespoons vegetable oil
2 medium green, red and/or yellow bell peppers, thinly sliced
1 small red onion, thinly sliced
1 package (1.25 ounces) ORTEGA® Taco Seasoning Mix
1 can (12 fluid ounces) evaporated milk
6 large eggs, lightly beaten
1 cup (4 ounces) shredded 4 cheese Mexican blend
12 (6-inch) fajita-size flour tortillas, warmed

Garnish Suggestions
ORTEGA Salsa, sour cream, additional cheese

HEAT oil in large nonstick skillet over medium-high heat. Add bell peppers, onion and seasoning mix; stir well. Cook, stirring frequently, for 3 to 5 minutes or until vegetables are crisp-tender. Transfer to bowl; cover.

COMBINE evaporated milk and eggs in medium bowl. Pour into heated skillet and scramble until soft curds form. Move eggs to center of skillet. Arrange vegetables around eggs. Sprinkle cheese over eggs and vegetables.

SERVE with tortillas. Garish as desired.

Makes 6 servings

Oven-Baked French Toast

12 slices cinnamon bread or cinnamon raisin bread
1 pint (16 ounces) half-and-half or light cream
2 eggs
6 tablespoons I CAN'T BELIEVE IT'S NOT BUTTER!® Spread, melted
2 tablespoons firmly packed brown sugar
2 teaspoons vanilla extract
1 teaspoon grated orange peel (optional)
¼ teaspoon ground cinnamon
⅛ teaspoon ground nutmeg (optional)

Preheat oven to 350°F.

In lightly greased 13×9-inch baking pan, arrange bread slices in two layers.

In large bowl, with wire whisk, blend remaining ingredients. Evenly pour over bread slices, pressing bread down until some liquid is absorbed and bread does not float. Bake 45 minutes or until center reaches 160°F. and bread is golden brown. Serve hot and sprinkle, if desired, with confectioners' sugar.

Makes 6 servings

Ortega® Huevos Rancheros

Broccoli, Potato & Bacon Egg Pie with Cheddar Cheese

    2 cups cooked broccoli florets
1½ cups cooked diced potatoes (about 2 medium)
1½ cups (lightly packed) grated CABOT® Sharp Cheddar Cheese (about 4 ounces)
    4 slices cooked bacon, chopped
    1 unbaked 9-inch deep-dish or 10-inch pie shell
    6 large eggs
    2 large egg yolks
1½ cups heavy cream
    1 teaspoon mild paprika
    ½ teaspoon salt
    ¼ teaspoon freshly ground black pepper

1. Preheat oven to 350°F.

2. Distribute broccoli, potatoes, cheese and bacon evenly in pie shell. In mixing bowl, whisk together whole eggs and egg yolks until well combined; add cream, paprika, salt and pepper and whisk again.

3. Pour cream mixture evenly over ingredients in pie shell. Bake for 30 to 40 minutes, or until golden on top and set all the way to center.   *Makes 6 to 8 servings*

Broccoli, Potato & Bacon Egg Pie with Cheddar Cheese

Ham & Asparagus Brunch Bake

2 boxes UNCLE BEN'S® Long Grain & Wild Rice Original Recipe
1 pound asparagus, cut into 1-inch pieces (about 2½ cups)
2 cups chopped ham
1 cup chopped yellow or red bell pepper
¼ cup finely chopped red onion
1 cup (4 ounces) shredded Swiss cheese

1. In large saucepan, prepare rice mixes according to package directions, adding asparagus during last 5 minutes of cooking.

2. Meanwhile, preheat oven to 350°F. Grease 11×7½-inch baking dish.

3. Remove rice mixture from heat. Add ham, bell pepper and onion; mix well. Place mixture in prepared baking dish; sprinkle with cheese.

4. Bake 25 to 30 minutes or until mixture is heated through.   *Makes 8 servings*

Variation: Substitute UNCLE BEN'S® Brand Butter & Herb Long Grain & Wild Rice for the Original Recipe Long Grain & Wild Rice.

Tip: This dish can be prepared ahead of time through step 3. Cover with foil and refrigerate several hours or overnight. Bake, covered, in preheated 350°F oven for 15 minutes. Remove foil and continue to bake until heated through, about 10 minutes.

SPAM™ Cakes

1½ cups pancake mix
1 cup milk
1 egg
1 tablespoon vegetable oil
1 (7-ounce) can SPAM® Classic, finely chopped
Syrup or honey

In large bowl, combine pancake mix, milk, egg and oil. Stir in SPAM®. Using ⅓ cup for each pancake, pour batter onto greased griddle; cook until browned on bottom. Turn and cook until browned. Serve with syrup or honey.   *Makes 6 servings (12 pancakes)*

Ham & Asparagus Brunch Bake

Summer Sausage 'n' Egg Wedges

  4 **eggs, beaten**
⅓ **cup milk**
¼ **cup all-purpose flour**
½ **teaspoon baking powder**
⅛ **teaspoon garlic powder**
2½ **cups (10 ounces) shredded Cheddar or mozzarella cheese, divided**
1½ **cups diced HILLSHIRE FARM® Summer Sausage**
  1 **cup cream-style cottage cheese with chives**

Preheat oven to 375°F.

Combine eggs, milk, flour, baking powder and garlic powder in medium bowl; beat until combined. Stir in 2 cups Cheddar cheese, Summer Sausage and cottage cheese. Pour into greased 9-inch pie plate. Bake, uncovered, 25 to 30 minutes or until golden and knife inserted into center comes out clean. To serve, cut into 6 wedges. Sprinkle wedges with remaining ½ cup Cheddar cheese.   *Makes 6 servings*

Farm Fresh Tip: Here's a simple do-ahead garlic bread and a great accompaniment to your favorite Hillshire Farm meal. Cut a 1-pound loaf of French bread into 1-inch slices. Spread with a mixture of ½ cup soft butter and ¼ teaspoon garlic powder. Sprinkle with salt, pepper and paprika. Reassemble the loaf and wrap in heavy-duty foil. Heat in a 350°F oven for 15 to 20 minutes.

Summer Sausage 'n' Egg Wedge

Breakfast Casserole

6 large eggs, beaten
½ cup sour cream
1 can (15 ounces) VEG•ALL® Original Mixed Vegetables, drained
1 cup frozen cubed hash brown potatoes, thawed
1 cup smoked sausage links, chopped
1 cup shredded pepper-jack cheese
2 tablespoons canned jalapeño pepper slices
1 cup broken tortilla chips

Preheat oven to 350°F.

In medium bowl, combine eggs and sour cream until smooth. Fold in remaining ingredients except tortilla chips.

Transfer mixture to greased 11×7-inch baking dish. Bake for 25 to 30 minutes or until eggs are set and puffed.

Top with tortilla chips and bake an additional 5 minutes. Serve with additional sour cream on the side, if desired.

Serve with fresh fruit for breakfast or brunch.   *Makes 6 to 8 servings*

Suggestion: For a milder flavor, substitute chopped fresh cilantro for the sliced jalapeño peppers.

Spicy Sausage Skillet Breakfast

2 bags SUCCESS® Rice
   Vegetable cooking spray
1 pound bulk turkey sausage
½ cup chopped onion
1 can (10 ounces) tomatoes with green chilies, undrained
1 tablespoon chili powder
1 cup (4 ounces) shredded reduced-fat Monterey Jack cheese

Prepare rice according to package directions.

Lightly spray large skillet with cooking spray. Crumble sausage into prepared skillet. Cook over medium heat until lightly browned, stirring occasionally. Add onion; cook until tender. Stir in tomatoes, chili powder and rice; simmer 2 minutes. Reduce heat to low. Simmer until no liquid remains, about 8 minutes, stirring occasionally. Sprinkle with cheese.   *Makes 6 to 8 servings*

Breakfast Casserole

Salads & Starters

Whether you want to tease appetites for a main course to come or make a meal of a healthy salad, you'll find the inspiration here. Mexican Shrimp Cocktail and Roasted Red Potato Bites look like fancy party fare you ordered from a caterer, but they are actually incredibly simple to put together. Indulge your salad cravings with Tuna-Papaya-Avocado Salad or Italian Antipasto Salad. When it comes to delicious starters, this chapter is the place to start.

Field Green Salad with Balsamic Vinaigrette (page 62)

41

Pizzette with Basil

1 can (6 ounces) CONTADINA® Italian Paste with Italian Seasonings
2 tablespoons softened cream cheese
2 tablespoons chopped fresh basil *or* 2 teaspoons dried basil leaves
1 loaf (1 pound) Italian bread, sliced ¼ inch thick
8 ounces mozzarella cheese, thinly sliced
   Whole basil leaves (optional)
   Freshly ground black pepper (optional)

1. Combine tomato paste, cream cheese and basil in small bowl.

2. Toast bread slices on *ungreased* baking sheet under broiler, 6 to 8 inches from heat, turning after 1 minute, until lightly browned on both sides; remove from broiler.

3. Spread 2 teaspoons tomato mixture onto each toasted bread slice; top with 1 slice (about ¼ ounce) mozzarella cheese.

4. Broil 6 to 8 inches from heat for 1 to 2 minutes or until cheese begins to melt. Top with whole basil leaves and pepper, if desired.   *Makes about 30 pizzas*

Prep Time: 7 minutes
Cook Time: 10 minutes

Pineapple Avocado Salad

2 cups fresh sliced pineapple cut into ½-inch pieces
¾ cup sliced avocado
¼ cup thinly sliced red onion
1 tablespoon finely chopped fresh oregano
   Ground black pepper
3 tablespoons fresh lime juice
1 teaspoon peanut or safflower oil
2 packets (4 teaspoons) NatraTaste® Brand Sugar Substitute
⅛ teaspoon salt
1 clove garlic, minced

1. Place pineapple on a plate and top with avocado, onion, oregano and pepper.

2. Combine remaining ingredients in a small jar with a lid. Shake, and using a spoon, drizzle dressing over salad.   *Makes 4 servings*

Pizzette with Basil

Easy Tossed Niçoise with Garlic and Cheese Dressing

1½ pounds steamed red potatoes, cut into small chunks
1 package (10 ounces) frozen Italian green beans, thawed and drained
¾ cup niçoise or pitted ripe olives, sliced
½ red onion, slivered
½ red bell pepper, slivered
½ green bell pepper, slivered
¼ cup coarsely chopped green onions, including tops
1½ cups Garlic and Cheese Dressing (recipe follows)
1 (7-ounce) STARKIST Flavor Fresh Pouch® Tuna (Albacore)
½ cup minced fresh parsley
Whole romaine leaves, washed and dried
Freshly ground black pepper (optional)
Grated Parmesan cheese (optional)

In large bowl, combine potatoes, beans, olives, red onion, bell peppers and green onions; toss with Garlic and Cheese Dressing. Refrigerate. Just before serving, add tuna and parsley. Line plates with lettuce; spoon salad onto leaves. Serve with black pepper and cheese, if desired.

Makes 6 to 8 servings

Garlic and Cheese Dressing

¼ cup wine vinegar
2 tablespoons lemon juice
1 to 2 cloves garlic, minced or pressed
1 tablespoon Dijon-style mustard
Salt and pepper to taste
1 cup olive oil
½ cup grated Parmesan cheese

In small bowl, whisk together vinegar, lemon juice, garlic, mustard, salt and pepper. Slowly add olive oil, whisking until all oil is added and dressing is thickened. Stir in cheese.

Easy Tossed Niçoise with Garlic and Cheese Dressing

Mexican Shrimp Cocktail

½ cup WISH-BONE® Italian Dressing*
½ cup chopped tomato
1 can (4 ounces) chopped green chilies, undrained
¼ cup chopped green onions
1½ teaspoons honey
¼ teaspoon hot pepper sauce
1 pound medium shrimp, cleaned and cooked
2 teaspoons finely chopped cilantro or parsley

Also terrific with WISH-BONE® Robusto Italian or Just 2 Good! Italian Dressing.

In medium bowl, combine Italian dressing, tomato, chilies, green onions, honey and hot pepper sauce. Stir in shrimp. Cover and marinate in refrigerator, stirring occasionally, at least 2 hours. Just before serving, stir in cilantro.   *Makes about 6 servings*

Home-Style Corn Cakes

1 cup yellow cornmeal
½ cup all-purpose flour
½ teaspoon baking powder
½ teaspoon baking soda
1 envelope LIPTON® RECIPE SECRETS® Onion Soup Mix*
¾ cup buttermilk
1 egg, beaten
1 can (14¾ ounces) cream-style corn
2 ounces roasted red peppers, chopped (about ¼ cup)
    I CAN'T BELIEVE IT'S NOT BUTTER!® Spread

Or, substitute LIPTON® RECIPE SECRETS® Golden Onion Soup Mix.

In large bowl, combine cornmeal, flour, baking powder and baking soda. Blend soup mix with buttermilk, egg, corn and roasted red peppers; stir into cornmeal mixture.

In 12-inch nonstick skillet or on griddle, melt ½ teaspoon Spread over medium heat. Drop ¼ cup batter for each corn cake and cook, turning once, 5 minutes or until cooked through and golden brown. Remove to serving platter and keep warm. Repeat with remaining batter and additional I Can't Believe It's Not Butter!® Spread if needed. Serve with sour cream and prepared salsa, if desired.   *Makes about 18 corn cakes*

Tip: Leftover corn cakes may be wrapped and frozen. Remove from wrapping and reheat straight from freezer in preheated 350°F oven for 15 minutes.

Mexican Shrimp Cocktail

California Cobb Salad with Lemon Aioli Dressing

¾ cup *French's® Gourmayo™* Caesar Ranch Mayonnaise
2 tablespoons lemon juice
2 tablespoons water
½ teaspoon finely minced garlic
12 cups mixed salad greens
1 cup grape tomatoes
4 hard cooked eggs, quartered
1 cup cubed avocado
½ cup crumbled cooked bacon
½ cup crumbled Gorgonzola, Roquefort or other blue cheese

1. Combine mayonnaise, lemon juice, water and garlic.

2. Arrange remaining ingredients on serving platter. Serve with dressing.   *Makes 4 servings*

Tip: Purchase salad greens and other components from the salad bar section of your supermarket. To make this an entrée salad, add cooked chicken, turkey or ham.

Prep Time: 20 minutes

California Cobb Salad with Lemon Aioli Dressing

Roasted Red Potato Bites

    1½ **pounds red potatoes (about 15 small)**
      1 **cup shredded cheddar cheese (about 4 ounces)**
    ½ **cup HELLMANN'S® or BEST FOODS® Real Mayonnaise**
    ½ **cup sliced green onions**
      2 **tablespoons chopped fresh basil leaves (optional)**
  10 **slices bacon, crisp-cooked and crumbled**

1. Preheat oven to 400°F. On large baking sheet, arrange potatoes and bake 35 minutes or until tender. Let stand until cool enough to handle.

2. Cut each potato in half, then cut thin slice from bottom of each potato half. With small melon baller or spoon, scoop pulp from potatoes leaving ¼-inch shell. Set aside shells and reserve pulp.

3. In medium bowl, lightly mash reserved pulp. Stir in remaining ingredients. Spoon or pipe potato filling into potato shells.

4. Arrange filled shells on baking sheet and broil 3 minutes or until golden and heated through.

Makes 30 bites

Salmon Broccoli Waldorf Salad

    1 **bag (16 ounces) BIRDS EYE® frozen Broccoli Cuts**
    1 **large Red Delicious apple, chopped**
  ¼ **cup thinly sliced green onions**
  ½ **cup bottled creamy roasted garlic, ranch or blue cheese dressing**
    1 **can (14¾ ounces) salmon, drained and flaked**

• In large saucepan, cook broccoli according to package directions; drain and rinse under cold water in colander.

• In large bowl, toss together broccoli, apple, onions and dressing. Gently stir in salmon; add pepper to taste.

Makes 4 servings

Pasta Waldorf Salad: Increase salad dressing to 1 cup. Add 6 cups cooked pasta with the salmon.

Serving Suggestion: Serve over lettuce leaves and sprinkle with toasted nuts.

Birds Eye Idea: To prevent cut fruits and vegetables, such as apples and artichokes, from discoloring, try rubbing them with a lemon wedge.

Roasted Red Potato Bites

Italian Antipasto Salad

  1 box (9 ounces) BIRDS EYE® frozen Deluxe Artichoke Heart Halves
  1 box (9 ounces) BIRDS EYE® frozen Deluxe Whole Green Beans
12 lettuce leaves
  1 pound salami, cut into ¾-inch cubes
 ¾ pound provolone cheese, cut into ¾-inch cubes
  1 jar (7 ounces) roasted red peppers*
 ⅓ cup Italian salad dressing

Or, substitute pimientos, drained and cut into thin strips.

• In large saucepan, cook artichokes and green beans according to package directions; drain. Rinse under cold water to cool; drain again.

• Place lettuce on serving platter. Arrange cooked vegetables, salami, cheese and peppers in separate piles.

• Drizzle with dressing just before serving.
                                                      Makes 6 servings

Serving Suggestion: Add pitted ripe olives and jarred peperoncini, if desired.

Birds Eye Idea: Don't discard the water after boiling vegetables. Use it for making soups, sauces or rice dishes to keep precious nutrients.

Prep Time: 5 minutes
Cook Time: 10 minutes

Italian Antipasto Salad

Caesar Salad in Crouton Cups

CRISCO® No-Stick Butter Flavor Spray
12 **slices white bread**
 1 **teaspoon garlic salt**
 1 **teaspoon thyme**
 1 **teaspoon rosemary**
 ½ **teaspoon cracked black pepper**
 4 **cups romaine lettuce, finely sliced into ⅛-inch strips**
 2 **green onions, thinly sliced, plus additional for garnish**
    Purchased Caesar dressing, to taste
    Shredded Parmesan cheese

Preheat oven to 350°F.

Spray 12-muffin pan with CRISCO Cooking Spray. Trim crusts off bread; spray both sides of bread with CRISCO Cooking Spray.

In a small bowl, mix together the garlic salt, thyme, rosemary and cracked pepper. Lightly sprinkle mixture over both sides of bread.

Use a rolling pin to slightly flatten bread and embed the spice mixture. Press each slice into a muffin cup, allowing edges to hang over cup.

Bake for 12 to 15 minutes or until golden brown and crisp. Remove from oven and cool. Toss lettuce and green onions with dressing. Spoon salad into Crouton Cups. Garnish with shredded Parmesan and green onion slices. Serve immediately.   *Makes 12 appetizer servings*

Prep Time: 10 minutes
Bake Time: 12 minutes

Caesar Salad in Crouton Cups

Mediterranean Orzo Salad

Salad

> 1 cup orzo pasta
> 1 cup diced red bell pepper
> ½ cup crumbled feta cheese
> 1 can (2¼ ounces) sliced ripe olives, rinsed and drained
> ¼ cup chopped fresh basil *or* ½ teaspoon dried basil
> Fresh basil leaves or parsley sprigs, for garnish (optional)

Salad Dressing

> 1 packet (1 ounce) HIDDEN VALLEY® The Original Ranch® Salad Dressing & Seasoning Mix
> 3 tablespoons olive oil
> 3 tablespoons red wine vinegar
> 1 teaspoon sugar

Cook orzo according to package directions, omitting salt. Rinse with cold water and drain well. Mix orzo, bell pepper, cheese, olives and chopped fresh basil in a large bowl. (If using dried basil, add to dressing.) Whisk together salad dressing & seasoning mix, oil, vinegar and sugar. Stir dressing into orzo mixture. Cover and refrigerate at least 2 hours. Garnish with basil leaves before serving, if desired.

Makes 4 to 6 servings

Pineapple Black Bean Salad

> 2 cups fresh DOLE® Tropical Gold® Pineapple, cut into chunks
> 1 can (14 to 16 ounces) black beans, rinsed and drained
> 1½ cups cooked brown rice
> 1½ cups cubed cooked chicken breast
> 1 medium DOLE® Red, Yellow or Green Bell Pepper, chopped
> ½ cup chopped DOLE® Celery
> ½ cup chopped green onions
> ½ cup fat-free or light honey Dijon salad dressing
> Cleaned and dried corn husks
> Hot peppers for garnish

• Combine pineapple chunks, beans, rice, chicken, bell pepper, celery and green onions in large serving bowl. Pour dressing over salad; toss to evenly coat. Serve in corn husks and garnish with peppers, if desired.

Makes 8 servings

Prep Time: 30 minutes

Mediterranean Orzo Salad

Sweet & Tangy Marinated Vegetables

   8 cups mixed fresh vegetables, such as broccoli, cauliflower, zucchini, carrots and red bell
        peppers, cut into 1- to 1½-inch pieces
   ⅓ cup distilled white vinegar
   ¼ cup sugar
   ¼ cup water
   1 packet (1 ounce) HIDDEN VALLEY® The Original Ranch® Salad Dressing & Seasoning Mix

Place vegetables in a gallon size Glad® Zipper Storage Bag. Whisk together vinegar, sugar, water and salad dressing & seasoning mix until sugar dissolves; pour over vegetables. Seal bag and shake to coat. Refrigerate 4 hours or overnight, turning bag occasionally.   *Makes 8 servings*

Note: Vegetables will keep up to 3 days in refrigerator.

Artichoke Wild Rice Salad

   1 jar (6 ounces) marinated artichoke hearts, undrained
   2 cups cooked wild rice
   1 cup frozen peas, thawed
   1 can (8 ounces) sliced water chestnuts, drained
   1 cup (4 ounces) shredded mozzarella cheese (optional)
   1 jar (2 ounces) diced pimiento, drained
   2 tablespoons canola oil
   1 tablespoon balsamic vinegar
   ½ teaspoon dried tarragon leaves
   ½ teaspoon Dijon mustard
   2 to 3 drops hot pepper sauce

1. Drain artichokes, reserving 2 tablespoons liquid.

2. Combine artichokes, rice, peas, water chestnuts, cheese and pimiento in large bowl. Combine oil, reserved liquid from artichokes, vinegar, tarragon, mustard and hot pepper sauce in small bowl; pour over rice mixture and toss. Refrigerate 4 hours or overnight to allow flavors to blend. Serve cold.   *Makes 6 to 8 servings*

Variation: Combine wild rice with white or brown rice. Cook the rices separately, since they have different cooking times, and combine them after cooking.

*Favorite recipe from **Minnesota Cultivated Wild Rice Council***

Grilled Potato Salad

1 envelope LIPTON® RECIPE SECRETS® Onion Soup Mix*
⅓ cup BERTOLLI® Olive Oil
2 tablespoons red wine vinegar
1 clove garlic, finely chopped
2 pounds small red or all-purpose potatoes, cut into 1-inch cubes
1 tablespoon fresh basil, chopped *or* 1 teaspoon dried basil leaves, crushed
    Freshly ground black pepper

Also terrific with LIPTON® RECIPE SECRETS® Onion Mushroom or Golden Onion Soup Mix.

1. In large bowl, blend soup mix, oil, vinegar and garlic; stir in potatoes.

2. Grease 30×18-inch sheet of heavy-duty aluminum foil; top with potato mixture. Wrap foil loosely around mixture, sealing edges airtight with double fold. Place on another sheet of 30×18-inch foil; seal edges airtight with double fold in opposite direction.

3. Grill, shaking package occasionally and turning package once, 40 minutes or until potatoes are tender. Spoon into serving bowl and toss with basil and pepper. Serve slightly warm or at room temperature.   *Makes 4 servings*

Oven Method: Preheat oven to 450°F. Prepare foil packet as above. Place in large baking pan on bottom rack and bake, turning packet once, 40 minutes or until potatoes are tender. Toss and serve as above.

Grilled Potato Salad

Field Green Salad with Balsamic Vinaigrette

    6 cups field greens (spring mix)
    1 cup mushrooms, thinly sliced
    ½ medium cucumber, thinly sliced
    ½ sweet onion, thinly sliced
        Balsamic Vinaigrette (recipe follows)
        Freshly grated Parmesan cheese to taste

In a large serving bowl, toss greens with mushrooms, cucumber and onion. Dress with Balsamic Vinaigrette as desired. Divide salad among 4 salad plates; garnish with Parmesan cheese. Serve immediately. Refrigerate any remaining dressing.   *Makes 4 servings*

Prep Time: 5 minutes

Balsamic Vinaigrette

    ¼ cup balsamic vinegar
    1 tablespoon Dijon mustard
    ¼ teaspoon sugar
    ¼ teaspoon salt
    ⅛ teaspoon pepper
    ¾ cup CRISCO® Canola Oil*

Or use your favorite Crisco Oil.

In small plastic container with tight-fitting lid, combine all ingredients except CRISCO Oil; shake well. Pour in CRISCO Oil and shake until well blended.   *Makes 4 servings*

Crab Cakes with Horseradish Mustard Sauce

½ cup mayonnaise
2 tablespoons *French's®* Honey Dijon Mustard
1 tablespoon prepared horseradish

Crab Cakes
1⅓ cups *French's®* French Fried Onions, divided
3 cans (6 ounces each) jumbo lump crabmeat, drained
¼ cup unseasoned dry bread crumbs
¼ cup mayonnaise
1 egg, slightly beaten
2 tablespoons chopped pimentos
2 tablespoons chopped fresh parsley
1 tablespoon *French's®* Honey Dijon Mustard
1 tablespoon prepared horseradish
1 teaspoon minced garlic

1. Combine ingredients for Horseradish Mustard Sauce in small bowl. Chill until ready to serve.

2. Lightly crush ⅔ *cup* French Fried Onions. Place in large bowl. Add remaining ingredients for crab cakes; mix until well combined. Shape mixture into cakes using about ¼ cup mixture for each; flatten slightly.

3. Heat *2 tablespoons oil* in 12-inch nonstick skillet over medium high heat. Cook crab cakes in batches, about 2 to 3 minutes per side or until golden. Drain. Transfer crab cakes to serving platter. Serve each crab cake topped with Horseradish Mustard Sauce and remaining onions.

Makes about 12 crab cakes

Prep Time: 15 minutes
Cook Time: 12 minutes

Pineapple Boats with Citrus Creme

1 large fresh DOLE® Tropical Gold® Pineapple
1 DOLE® Banana, peeled, sliced
1 orange, peeled, sliced
1 apple, cored, sliced
1 DOLE® Pear, cored, sliced
1 cup seedless DOLE® Grapes (red and green)

Citrus Creme
1 cup vanilla nonfat yogurt
2 tablespoons brown sugar
1 tablespoon minced crystallized ginger, optional
1 teaspoon grated orange peel
1 teaspoon grated lime peel

• Cut pineapple in half lengthwise through the crown. Cut fruit from shells, leaving shells intact. Core and chunk fruit.

• Combine pineapple chunks with remaining fruit. Spoon into pineapple boats.

• Combine all ingredients for Citrus Creme. Serve with pineapple boats.   *Makes 8 servings*

Prep Time: 20 minutes

Pineapple Boat with Citrus Creme

Tuna-Papaya-Avocado Salad

1 (3-ounce) STARKIST Flavor Fresh Pouch® Tuna (Albacore or Chunk Light)
   Lettuce leaves
½ ripe papaya, peeled, seeded and thinly sliced
¼ medium-ripe avocado, peeled, pitted and thinly sliced

Dressing
2 tablespoons orange juice
1 tablespoon vegetable or olive oil
1 teaspoon honey
   Dash pepper
   Strawberry or orange wedges for garnish (optional)

Mound tuna in center of lettuce-lined plate. Surround with slices of papaya and avocado. For dressing, in a small shaker jar combine orange juice, oil, honey and pepper. Cover and shake until well blended. Drizzle over salad. Garnish with strawberry if desired.   *Makes 1 serving*

Note: You can substitute ripe pears, peaches or plums for the papaya.

Prep Time: 10 minutes

California Crab Salad

1 packet (0.4 ounce) HIDDEN VALLEY® The Original Ranch® Buttermilk Recipe
   Salad Dressing Mix
1 cup buttermilk
1 cup mayonnaise
1 tablespoon grated fresh ginger
1 teaspoon prepared horseradish
2 cups cooked white rice, chilled
4 lettuce leaves
8 ounces cooked crabmeat, chilled
1 large ripe avocado, thinly sliced
½ medium cucumber, thinly sliced

In medium bowl, whisk together salad dressing mix, buttermilk and mayonnaise. Whisk in ginger and horseradish. Cover and refrigerate 30 minutes. To serve, arrange ½ cup rice on top of each lettuce leaf. Top with 2 tablespoons of the dressing. Arrange one-quarter of the crabmeat, avocado and cucumber on top of each rice mound. Serve with remaining dressing. Garnish with cherry tomatoes and lime wedges, if desired.   *Makes 4 servings*

Tuna-Papaya-Avocado Salad

Crab and Artichoke Stuffed Mushrooms

½ pound Florida blue crab meat
1 (14-ounce) can artichoke hearts, drained and finely chopped
1 cup mayonnaise*
½ cup grated Parmesan cheese
¼ teaspoon lemon pepper seasoning
⅛ teaspoon salt
⅛ teaspoon cayenne pepper
30 large fresh Florida mushrooms

Or, you can substitute a mixture of ½ cup mayonnaise and ½ cup plain yogurt.

Remove any pieces of shell or cartilage from crab meat. Combine crab meat, artichoke hearts, mayonnaise, Parmesan cheese and seasonings; mix until well blended. Remove stems from mushrooms and fill the caps with crab meat mixture. Place in a lightly oiled, shallow baking dish. Bake in a preheated 400°F oven for 10 minutes or until hot and bubbly.

Makes 30 appetizer servings

*Favorite recipe from **Florida Department of Agriculture and Consumer Services, Bureau of Seafood and Aquaculture***

Grilled Shrimp Salad with Hot Bacon Vinaigrette

4 strips bacon, chopped
½ cup prepared Italian or vinaigrette salad dressing
⅓ cup *French's®* Honey Dijon Mustard or *French's®* Sweet & Tangy Honey Mustard
2 tablespoons water
8 cups mixed salad greens
1 cup diced yellow bell peppers
1 cup halved cherry tomatoes
½ cup pine nuts
1 pound jumbo or extra large shrimp, shelled with tails left on

1. Cook bacon until crisp in medium skillet. Whisk in salad dressing, mustard and water; keep warm over very low heat.

2. Place salad greens, bell peppers, tomatoes and pine nuts in large bowl; toss. Arrange on salad plates.

3. Cook shrimp in an electric grill pan or barbecue grill 3 minutes until pink. Arrange on salads, dividing evenly. Serve with dressing.

Makes 4 servings

Crab and Artichoke Stuffed Mushrooms

Soups & Sides

Great go-withs can really make a meal. Choose from recipes for hearty soups, such as the Easy Tomato Minestrone pictured here, or be adventurous and try Chilled Fire Gazpacho, a spicy hot soup served ice cold. Don't forget to bring back some of the old-fashioned favorites that are true traditions—what would a family holiday feast be without French's® Original Green Bean Casserole or Creamed Spinach à la Lawry's®? With the deliciously easy recipes you'll find here, you may not even need a main course.

Cheddar Baked Potatoes

1 jar (1 pound) RAGÚ® Cheesy! Double Cheddar Sauce
1 bag (16 ounces) frozen vegetables, cooked and drained
6 large baking potatoes, unpeeled and baked

In 2-quart saucepan, heat Sauce. Stir in vegetables; heat through.

Cut a lengthwise slice from top of each potato. Lightly mash pulp in each potato. Evenly spoon sauce mixture onto each potato. Sprinkle, if desired, with ground black pepper.

Makes 6 servings

Prep Time: 20 minutes
Cook Time: 10 minutes

Golden Gate Wild Rice Cioppino

2 cups chopped onions
1 medium green bell pepper, chopped
4 cloves garlic, minced
2 tablespoons olive oil
1 cup white wine
1 can (28 ounces) whole tomatoes, drained and chopped
1 bottle (8 ounces) clam juice
1 bay leaf
½ teaspoon dried basil leaves
½ teaspoon dried oregano leaves
½ teaspoon dried rosemary
¼ teaspoon red pepper flakes
2 cups cooked California wild rice
6 large *or* 12 small clams, well scrubbed
½ pound medium shrimp, peeled and deveined
½ pound scallops, cut into halves crosswise
    Chopped parsley

In large stockpot or Dutch oven, sauté onions, bell pepper and garlic in oil until onion is soft. Add wine, tomatoes, clam juice, bay leaf, basil, oregano, rosemary and pepper flakes. Bring to a boil, reduce heat and simmer 30 minutes, stirring often. Add rice and bring to a simmer. Add clams; cook until clams open. Discard any clams that do not open. Add shrimp and scallops; cook until shrimp turns pink, about 2 to 3 minutes; do not overcook. Sprinkle with parsley.

Makes 4 servings

Favorite recipe from **California Wild Rice Advisory Board**

Cheddar Baked Potato

Chilled Fire Gazpacho

1½ **cups tomato juice**
⅓ **cup extra-virgin olive oil**
¼ **cup fresh lime juice**
6 **medium ripe tomatoes, coarsely chopped (about 5 cups)**
1 **medium cucumber, coarsely chopped**
1 **red bell pepper, coarsely chopped**
2 **large green onions, coarsely chopped**
2 **tablespoons chopped fresh parsley**
2 **teaspoons TABASCO® brand Pepper Sauce**
½ **teaspoon salt**

Combine tomato juice, olive oil and lime juice in medium bowl. Purée tomatoes, cucumber, red bell pepper and green onions in small batches in food processor or blender, adding tomato juice mixture gradually. (Do not purée completely; soup should retain some crunch.) Stir in parsley, TABASCO® Sauce and salt. Chill until ready to serve.

To serve, ladle gazpacho into chilled soup bowls or mugs. Serve with additional TABASCO® Sauce, if desired.
Makes 6 servings

Garlic Mashed Potatoes

6 **medium all-purpose potatoes, peeled, if desired, and cut into chunks (about 3 pounds)**
Water
1 **envelope LIPTON® RECIPE SECRETS® Savory Herb with Garlic Soup Mix***
½ **cup milk**
½ **cup I CAN'T BELIEVE IT'S NOT BUTTER!® Spread**

*Also terrific with LIPTON® RECIPE SECRETS® Onion or Golden Onion Soup Mix.

1. In 4-quart saucepan, cover potatoes with water; bring to a boil.

2. Reduce heat to low and simmer uncovered 20 minutes or until potatoes are very tender; drain.

3. Return potatoes to saucepan, then mash. Stir in remaining ingredients.   *Makes 8 servings*

Chilled Fire Gazpacho

Broccoli Casserole with Crumb Topping

2 slices day-old white bread, coarsely crumbled (about 1¼ cups)
½ cup shredded mozzarella cheese (about 2 ounces)
2 tablespoons chopped fresh parsley (optional)
2 tablespoons BERTOLLI® Olive Oil, divided
1 clove garlic, finely chopped
6 cups broccoli florets and/or cauliflowerets
1 envelope LIPTON® RECIPE SECRETS® Onion Soup Mix
1 cup water
1 large tomato, chopped

1. In small bowl, combine bread crumbs, cheese, parsley, if desired, 1 tablespoon oil and garlic; set aside.

2. In 12-inch skillet, heat remaining 1 tablespoon oil over medium heat and cook broccoli, stirring frequently, 2 minutes.

3. Stir in onion soup mix blended with water. Bring to a boil over high heat. Reduce heat to low and simmer uncovered, stirring occasionally, 8 minutes or until broccoli is almost tender. Add tomato and simmer 2 minutes.

4. Spoon vegetable mixture into 1½-quart casserole; top with bread crumb mixture. Broil 1½ minutes or until crumbs are golden and cheese is melted. *Makes 6 servings*

Broccoli Casserole with Crumb Topping

Hearty 3-Bean & Ham Soup

1 cup chopped onion
1 tablespoon vegetable or olive oil
1 (15-ounce) can *each* pinto beans, black beans and red kidney beans, drained and rinsed
1 cup sliced carrots
3½ cups water
4 cubes HERB-OX® beef bouillon
1 (14½-ounce) can diced tomatoes
⅓ cup chili sauce
3 tablespoons cider vinegar
1 tablespoon firmly packed brown sugar
2 teaspoons Worcestershire sauce
2 teaspoons prepared mustard
1 cup diced ham
2 tablespoons chopped fresh parsley

In large saucepan, sauté onion in oil until golden. Stir in beans and next 9 ingredients. Bring mixture to a boil. Reduce heat, cover and simmer for 25 to 30 minutes or until carrots are tender. Stir in ham and parsley. Ladle into bowls and serve. *Makes 6 to 8 servings*

Santa Fe Tomato Chowder

1 tablespoon butter or margarine
2 teaspoons minced garlic
4 ripe tomatoes, chopped
1 can (15 ounces) tomato sauce
1 cup frozen corn kernels
¼ cup chopped fresh cilantro
1 tablespoon *Frank's® RedHot®* Original Cayenne Pepper Sauce
½ teaspoon chili powder
1 ripe avocado, peeled and chopped
1 cup (4 ounces) shredded Monterey Jack cheese
1⅓ cups *French's®* French Fried Onions

1. Melt butter in large saucepan; sauté garlic for 1 minute. Add tomatoes and cook 5 minutes. Stir in 1 cup water, tomato sauce, corn, cilantro, *Frank's RedHot* Sauce and chili powder.

2. Bring to a boil over high heat. Reduce heat; simmer 10 minutes. Spoon soup into serving bowls; sprinkle with avocado, cheese and French Fried Onions. *Makes 4 servings*

Hearty 3-Bean & Ham Soup

Stuffed Portobello Mushrooms

1 box UNCLE BEN'S® Long Grain & Wild Rice Roasted Garlic
2 tablespoons prepared pesto sauce
8 ounces cream cheese, softened
4 large portobello mushrooms
   Salt and black pepper to taste
1 large tomato
4 tablespoons grated Parmesan cheese
4 basil leaves (optional)

COOK: Preheat oven to 400°F. CLEAN: Wash hands. Prepare rice according to package directions. Meanwhile, stir pesto into cream cheese until well blended. Remove stems from mushrooms. Clean mushroom caps well. Place mushrooms, stem side up, on baking sheet. Sprinkle with salt and pepper. Spread one fourth of cream cheese mixture onto each mushroom. Top with ½ cup cooked rice. Slice tomato into 4 thick slices. Place 1 slice on top of rice and sprinkle each mushroom with 1 tablespoon Parmesan cheese. Bake 10 minutes.

SERVE: Serve each mushroom on a separate plate and garnish with basil leaf, if desired.

CHILL: Refrigerate leftovers immediately.

Makes 4 servings

Cook Time: 30 minutes

Classic Onion Soup

4 large yellow onions (about 9 to 11 ounces each), sliced
6 tablespoons butter or margarine
1 tablespoon sugar
2 quarts (8 cups) reduced-sodium chicken broth
½ cup brandy (optional)
   Salt and black pepper to taste
½ baguette French bread, cut into slices and toasted
   Grated Romano cheese

Melt butter in 4-quart saucepan or Dutch oven. Add onions; cook over medium heat 12 minutes, stirring often, or until tender and golden. Add sugar and cook, stirring for 1 minute. Add broth; cover and bring to a boil. Reduce heat; simmer 12 minutes. If desired, add brandy; cook 2 minutes longer. Season with salt and pepper. To serve, ladle soup into bowl; float toast on top. Sprinkle with cheese.

Makes 6 servings

Favorite recipe from **National Onion Association**

Stuffed Portobello Mushroom

Original Ranch® Roasted Potatoes

2 pounds small red potatoes, quartered
¼ cup vegetable oil
1 packet (1 ounce) HIDDEN VALLEY® The Original Ranch® Salad Dressing & Seasoning Mix

Place potatoes in a gallon-size Glad® Zipper Storage Bag. Pour oil over potatoes. Seal bag and toss to coat. Add salad dressing & seasoning mix; seal bag and toss again until coated. Bake in ungreased baking pan at 450°F for 30 to 35 minutes or until potatoes are brown and crisp.

Makes 4 to 6 servings

Vegetable Gratin

2 tablespoons olive oil
3 small *or* 1 large zucchini, cut into ¼-inch slices
⅛ teaspoon salt, divided
⅛ teaspoon thyme, divided
⅛ teaspoon rosemary, divided
⅛ teaspoon freshly ground black pepper, divided
1 (6.5-ounce) package ALOUETTE® Savory Vegetable
2 cups fresh broccoli florets
2 small yellow squash, sliced
1 small onion, sliced
1 cup crushed BRETON® Wheat Crackers

• Preheat oven to 350°F. Place oil in medium-sized gratin or shallow baking dish.

• Layer zucchini in prepared dish.

• Sprinkle zucchini lightly with half each of salt, thyme, rosemary and pepper.

• Place 3 tablespoons Alouette on top of zucchini.

• Layer with broccoli, yellow squash, onion, remaining seasonings and Alouette until dish is filled.

• Sprinkle with cracker crumbs; cover with foil. Bake 20 minutes.

• Remove foil; bake another 20 minutes. Brown lightly under broiler 1 to 2 minutes. Serve hot or at room temperature.　　　　　*Makes 6 to 8 servings*

Note: This gratin is a delicious way to liven up vegetables! It's great with grilled chicken or steak.

Wisconsin Sausage Soup

½ cup butter
1 onion, chopped
1 carrot, chopped
1 teaspoon minced garlic
1 cup all-purpose flour
2 cups chicken broth
2 cups milk
¾ cup beer
1 teaspoon Worcestershire sauce
½ teaspoon salt
½ teaspoon dry mustard
1 bay leaf
7 ounces Cheddar cheese, shredded
3 ounces Swiss cheese, shredded
½ pound HILLSHIRE FARM® Smoked Sausage

Melt butter in medium saucepan over medium heat. Add onion, carrot and garlic; sauté until softened. Add flour; cook 5 minutes, stirring often. Add chicken broth, milk, beer, Worcestershire sauce, salt, mustard and bay leaf. Reduce heat to low; cook until soup has thickened, whisking often. Remove and discard bay leaf.

Slowly whisk cheeses into soup until blended and smooth. Cut Smoked Sausage lengthwise into quarters, then slice into ½-inch pieces. Sauté sausage in small skillet over medium-high heat until heated through. Blot excess grease with paper towels; add sausage to soup. Serve soup hot.

Makes 8 to 10 servings

Wisconsin Sausage Soup

Mexican-Style Stuffed Peppers

8 medium green bell peppers, halved and seeded
3 cups cooked long-grain white rice
1 package (10 ounces) frozen peas and carrots
1 cup whole kernel corn
½ cup chopped green onions
1¾ cups ORTEGA® Salsa-Homestyle Recipe, divided
1½ cups 4-cheese Mexican blend, divided

PREHEAT oven to 375°F.

PLACE bell peppers in microwave-safe dish with 3 tablespoons water. Cover with plastic wrap. Microwave on HIGH (100%) power for 4 to 5 minutes or until slightly tender. Drain.

COMBINE rice, peas and carrots, corn, green onions, ¾ cup salsa and 1 cup cheese in large bowl. Fill each pepper with about ½ cup rice mixture. Place peppers in ungreased 13×9×2-inch baking dish; top with remaining salsa and cheese.

BAKE uncovered for 20 to 25 minutes. Uncover; bake for additional 5 minutes or until heated through and cheese is melted. *Makes 8 servings*

Green Beans with Toasted Pecans

3 tablespoons I CAN'T BELIEVE IT'S NOT BUTTER!® Spread, melted
1 teaspoon sugar
¼ teaspoon LAWRY'S® Garlic Powder with Parsley
Pinch ground red pepper
Salt to taste
⅓ cup chopped pecans
1 pound green beans

In small bowl, blend I Can't Believe It's Not Butter!® Spread, sugar, garlic powder, pepper and salt.

In 12-inch nonstick skillet, heat 2 teaspoons garlic mixture over medium-high heat and cook pecans, stirring frequently, 2 minutes or until pecans are golden. Remove pecans and set aside.

In same skillet, heat remaining garlic mixture and stir in green beans. Cook, covered, over medium heat, stirring occasionally, 6 minutes or until green beans are tender. Stir in pecans.
Makes 4 servings

Tortilla Soup

   1 tablespoon butter or margarine
  ½ cup chopped green bell pepper
  ½ cup chopped onion
  ½ teaspoon ground cumin
3½ cups (two 14½-ounce cans) chicken broth
   1 jar (16 ounces) ORTEGA® Salsa-Thick & Chunky
   1 cup whole-kernel corn
   1 tablespoon vegetable oil
   6 corn tortillas, cut into ½-inch strips
  ¾ cup (3 ounces) shredded 4-cheese Mexican blend
    Sour cream (optional)

MELT butter in medium saucepan over medium heat. Add bell pepper, onion and cumin; cook for 3 to 4 minutes or until tender. Stir in broth, salsa and corn. Bring to a boil. Reduce heat to low; cook for 5 minutes.

HEAT vegetable oil in medium skillet over medium-high heat. Add tortilla strips; cook for 3 to 4 minutes or until crisp.

SERVE in soup bowls. Top with tortilla strips, cheese and a dollop of sour cream.

Makes 6 servings

Albacore Corn Chowder

  2 tablespoons butter or margarine
  ¾ cup chopped carrot
  ½ cup sliced celery
  ½ cup chopped onion
  2 to 3 tablespoons flour
  1 teaspoon dried thyme or Italian seasoning
  1 can (17 ounces) cream-style corn
  2 cups milk
  1 (7-ounce) STARKIST Flavor Fresh Pouch® Tuna (Albacore)
  1 cup water
  1 teaspoon chicken flavor instant bouillon

In medium saucepan, melt butter over medium heat; sauté carrot, celery and onion about 3 minutes. Add flour and thyme; blend well. Cook 3 more minutes. Add corn, milk, tuna, water and bouillon, stirring to blend. Cover and simmer (do not boil) 5 minutes to heat through, stirring occasionally.

Makes 4 servings

Tortilla Soup

Rosemary Roasted Oven Fries

CRISCO® No-Stick Cooking Spray
3 large baking potatoes
¼ cup CRISCO® Vegetable Oil*
2 teaspoons dried rosemary
1 teaspoon salt
⅛ teaspoon pepper
¼ cup grated Parmesan cheese
Ranch or blue cheese dressing for dipping, optional

Or use your favorite Crisco Oil.

Preheat oven to 450°F.

Spray baking sheet with CRISCO Cooking Spray; set aside.

Slice potatoes into ½-inch wedges; rinse with cold water and pat dry.

Whisk together CRISCO Oil, rosemary, salt and pepper in medium bowl. Add potato wedges; toss to coat. Place potato wedges on prepared baking sheet; bake 45 minutes, turning every 15 minutes. Remove from oven; sprinkle with Parmesan cheese.

Serve immediately with your choice of dressing for dipping.   *Makes 4 to 6 servings*

Prep Time: 10 minutes
Cook Time: 45 minutes

Savory Beets

2 tablespoons chopped onion
1 tablespoon butter or margarine
3 tablespoons honey
2 tablespoons red or white wine vinegar
Salt to taste
⅛ teaspoon ground cloves
1 can (16 ounces) sliced beets, drained

Sauté onion in butter in large skillet over medium heat until softened. Add honey, vinegar, salt and cloves; cook and stir until mixture begins to boil. Add beets; cook until thoroughly heated.

Makes 4 servings

Favorite recipe from **National Honey Board**

Rosemary Roasted Oven Fries

Avocado Ranch Soup

   1 can (14½ ounces) chicken broth
   1 cup milk
   ¾ cup plain lowfat yogurt
   ¼ cup mayonnaise
   1 packet (1 ounce) HIDDEN VALLEY® The Original Ranch® Salad Dressing & Seasoning Mix
   1 large ripe avocado, cut into chunks
   1 medium tomato, diced
   ½ unpared cucumber, seeded and diced
   ¼ cup finely diced purple onion
     Avocado slices

In blender, combine chicken broth, milk, yogurt, mayonnaise, salad dressing & seasoning mix and avocado chunks. Purée until smooth. Pour mixture into large bowl. Stir in tomato, cucumber and onion. Cover and refrigerate at least 4 hours. Garnish each bowl with avocado slices before serving.
Makes 6 servings

Easy Tomato Minestrone

   3 slices bacon, diced
   ½ cup chopped onion
   1 large clove garlic, minced
 3½ cups water
   2 cans (10½ ounces each) beef broth, undiluted
   1 can (15 ounces) Great Northern beans, undrained
   1 can (6 ounces) CONTADINA® Tomato Paste
   ¼ cup chopped fresh parsley
   1 teaspoon dried oregano leaves, crushed
   1 teaspoon dried basil leaves, crushed
   ¼ teaspoon pepper
   ½ cup dry pasta shells, macaroni or vermicelli, broken into 1-inch pieces
   1 package (16 ounces) frozen mixed Italian vegetables
   ½ cup grated Parmesan cheese (optional)

1. Sauté bacon, onion and garlic in large saucepan until onion is translucent.

2. Stir in water, broth, beans and liquid, tomato paste, parsley, oregano, basil, pepper and pasta; heat to boiling.

3. Reduce heat; simmer 15 minutes. Mix in vegetables; cook additional 10 minutes. Serve with Parmesan cheese, if desired.
Makes about 8 servings

Avocado Ranch Soup

Creamed Spinach à la Lawry's®

2 packages (10 ounces each) frozen spinach, cooked and drained
4 slices bacon
1 small onion, minced
2 cloves garlic, minced
2 tablespoons all-purpose flour
1 teaspoon LAWRY'S® Seasoned Salt
½ teaspoon freshly ground black pepper, or to taste
2 cups milk

Drain spinach well and squeeze out excess moisture with hands; chop finely and set aside. Fry bacon in heavy skillet until crisp; remove, drain and chop. Sauté onion and garlic in bacon drippings; add flour, Lawry's® Seasoned Salt and pepper and blend thoroughly. Slowly add milk, stirring constantly until thickened. Add spinach and bacon; heat.   *Makes 4 servings*

Meal Idea: Serve with prime rib or roast beef.

Prep Time: 15 minutes
Cook Time: 20 minutes

Original Green Bean Casserole

1 can (10¾ ounces) condensed cream of mushroom soup
¾ cup milk
⅛ teaspoon ground black pepper
2 packages (9 ounces each) frozen cut green beans, thawed and drained *or* 2 cans
      (14½ ounces each) cut green beans, drained
1⅓ cups *French's*® French Fried Onions, divided

Preheat oven to 350°F. Combine soup, milk and ground pepper in 1½-quart casserole; stir until well blended. Stir in beans and ⅔ *cup* French Fried Onions.

Bake, uncovered, 30 minutes or until hot. Stir; sprinkle with remaining ⅔ *cup* onions. Bake 5 minutes or until onions are golden.   *Makes 6 servings*

Microwave Directions: Prepare green bean mixture as above; pour into 1½-quart microwave-safe casserole. Cook, covered, on HIGH 8 to 10 minutes or until heated through. Stir beans halfway through cooking time. Top with remaining French Fried Onions; cook, uncovered, 1 minute. Let stand 5 minutes.

Prep Time: 5 minutes
Cook Time: 35 minutes

Creamed Spinach à la Lawry's®

Manhattan Clam Chowder

  2 pieces bacon, diced
  1 large red bell pepper, diced
  1 large green bell pepper, diced
  1 rib celery, chopped
  1 carrot, peeled and chopped
  1 small onion, chopped
  1 clove garlic, finely chopped
  2 cups bottled clam juice
  1 cup CLAMATO® Tomato Cocktail
  2 medium potatoes, peeled and diced
  1 large tomato, chopped
  1 teaspoon oregano
  ½ teaspoon black pepper
  2 cups fresh or canned clams, chopped (about 24 shucked clams)

In heavy 4-quart saucepan, sauté bacon, bell peppers, celery, carrot, onion and garlic over medium heat until tender, about 10 minutes. (Do not brown bacon.) Add clam juice, Clamato, potatoes, tomato, oregano and black pepper. Simmer 35 minutes or until potatoes are tender. Add clams; cook 5 minutes more.
Makes 8 servings

Italian Bow Tie Vegetable Soup

  3 cans (14½ ounces each) chicken broth
  1 can (14½ ounces) Italian-style or regular stewed tomatoes
  ½ teaspoon Italian seasoning
1½ cups (4 ounces) uncooked bow tie pasta (farfalle)
  1 package (about 1 pound) small frozen precooked meatballs
  1 medium zucchini, cut into ¼-inch slices
  ½ cup diced red or green bell pepper
1½ cups *French's*® French Fried Onions

1. Combine broth, tomatoes and Italian seasoning in large saucepan. Bring to a boil.

2. Stir in pasta, meatballs, zucchini and bell pepper. Simmer for 12 minutes or until pasta is cooked al dente and meatballs are heated through, stirring occasionally. Spoon soup into serving bowls; top with French Fried Onions.
Makes 6 servings

Prep Time: 5 minutes
Cook Time: 12 minutes

Manhattan Clam Chowder

1-2-3 Steak Soup

1 pound boneless beef sirloin steak, cut into 1-inch cubes
1 tablespoon vegetable oil
½ pound sliced mushrooms (about 2½ cups)
2 cups *French's*® French Fried Onions, divided
1 package (16 ounces) frozen vegetables for stew (potatoes, carrots, celery and pearl onions)
2 cans (14½ ounces each) beef broth
1 can (8 ounces) tomato sauce
1 tablespoon *French's*® Worcestershire Sauce
   Garnish: chopped parsley (optional)

1. Cook beef in hot oil in large saucepan over medium heat until browned, stirring frequently. Remove beef from pan; set aside.

2. Sauté mushrooms and ⅔ *cup* French Fried Onions in drippings in same pan over medium heat until golden, stirring occasionally. Stir in vegetables, broth, tomato sauce and Worcestershire. Return beef to pan.

3. Heat to a boil over high heat; reduce heat to low. Cover and simmer 20 minutes or until vegetables are tender, stirring occasionally. Spoon soup into serving bowls; top with remaining onions. Garnish with chopped parsley, if desired. *Makes 8 servings*

Prep Time: 5 minutes
Cook Time: 30 minutes

Simple Suppers

A simple meal shared with family or friends always brings out the best in the food and the guests. You'll find recipes here from some of your favorite brand names that require very little time to make and use clever shortcuts. Creamy Chicken & Linguini or Ragú® Pizza Burgers are only a few of the family pleasers that can be on the table in about 30 minutes or even less. One look at these mouthwatering pasta, chicken, beef and fish dishes and you might be tempted to throw away those take-out menus.

Tortellini Bake Parmesano
(page 114)

Caribbean Pork Kabobs and Rice

    1 cup UNCLE BEN'S® ORIGINAL CONVERTED® Brand Rice
1½ cups peeled, diced sweet potato
    2 tablespoons plus 2 teaspoons Caribbean seasoning, divided
    1 can (8 ounces) pineapple chunks in juice
    1 (12-ounce) pork tenderloin, cut into 1½-inch cubes
    1 red bell pepper, cut into 1-inch squares
    1 green bell pepper, cut into 1-inch squares
   ¼ cup dry-roasted peanuts

1. In medium pan, heat 2 cups water to a boil. Add rice, sweet potato and 2 teaspoons Caribbean seasoning. Cover, reduce heat and simmer 10 minutes or until rice and sweet potato are tender.

2. Drain pineapple chunks, reserving juice. Add pineapple chunks to rice mixture.

3. Preheat broiler. Place remaining 2 tablespoons Caribbean seasoning into large resealable plastic food storage bag. Add pork; seal bag and turn to coat pork with seasoning. Thread pork and bell peppers onto skewers.

4. Broil kabobs 4 minutes on each side. Turn and brush with reserved pineapple juice. Continue cooking 2 minutes on each side until pork is no longer pink.

5. Top rice with peanuts and serve with kabobs.

Makes 4 servings

Hearty Ground Beef Stew

    1 pound ground beef
    3 cloves garlic, minced
    1 package (16 ounces) Italian-style frozen vegetables
    2 cups southern-style hash brown potatoes
    1 jar (14 ounces) marinara sauce
    1 can (10½ ounces) condensed beef broth, undiluted
    3 tablespoons *French's*® Worcestershire Sauce

1. Brown beef with garlic in large saucepan; drain. Add remaining ingredients. Heat to boiling. Cover. Reduce heat to medium-low. Cook 10 minutes or until vegetables are crisp-tender.

2. Serve in warm bowls with garlic bread, if desired.

Makes 6 servings

Prep Time: 5 minutes
Cook Time: 15 minutes

Caribbean Pork Kabobs and Rice

Ragú® Pizza Burgers

   1 **pound ground beef**
   2 **cups RAGÚ® Old World Style® Pasta Sauce, divided**
   1 **cup shredded mozzarella cheese (about 4 ounces), divided**
  ¼ **teaspoon salt**
   6 **English muffins, split and toasted**

1. In small bowl, combine ground beef, ½ cup Ragú Pasta Sauce, ½ cup cheese and salt. Shape into 6 patties. Grill or broil until done.

2. Meanwhile, heat remaining pasta sauce. To serve, arrange burgers on muffin halves. Top with remaining cheese, sauce and muffin halves. *Makes 6 servings*

Prep Time: 10 minutes
Cook Time: 15 minutes

Savory Pork & Apple Stir-Fry

   1 **package (7.2 ounces) RICE-A-RONI® Rice Pilaf**
1⅓ **cups apple juice or apple cider, divided**
   1 **pound boneless pork loin, pork tenderloin or skinless, boneless chicken breast halves**
   1 **teaspoon paprika**
   1 **teaspoon dried thyme leaves**
  ½ **teaspoon ground sage or poultry seasoning**
  ½ **teaspoon salt (optional)**
   2 **tablespoons margarine or butter**
   2 **medium apples, cored and sliced**
   1 **teaspoon cornstarch**
  ⅓ **cup coarsely chopped walnuts**

1. Prepare Rice-A-Roni® Mix as package directs, substituting 1 cup water and 1 cup apple juice for water in directions.

2. While Rice-A-Roni® is simmering, cut pork into 1½×¼-inch strips. Combine seasonings; toss with meat.

3. In second large skillet, melt margarine over medium heat. Stir-fry meat 3 to 4 minutes or just until pork is no longer pink.

4. Add apples; stir-fry 2 to 3 minutes or until apples are almost tender. Add combined remaining ⅓ cup apple juice and cornstarch. Stir-fry 1 to 2 minutes or until thickened to form glaze.

5. Stir in nuts. Serve rice topped with pork mixture. *Makes 4 servings*

Ragú® Pizza Burgers

Mariachi Chicken

1¼ cups crushed tortilla chips
1 package (1 ounce) LAWRY'S® Taco Spices & Seasonings
2 dozen chicken drummettes or 1 pound boneless chicken breasts
Salsa and sour cream (optional)

In large resealable plastic bag, combine chips and Taco Spices & Seasonings. Dampen chicken with water; shake off excess. Place a few pieces at a time in bag; seal and shake to coat with chips. Arrange in greased shallow baking pan. Bake, uncovered, in preheated 350°F oven for 40 to 45 minutes, until chicken is thoroughly cooked. Serve with salsa and sour cream, if desired.

Makes 4 main-dish servings or 24 appetizers

Meal Idea: Serve with Mexican rice and/or refried beans and a crisp green salad or coleslaw.

Prep Time: 5 to 10 minutes
Cook Time: 40 to 45 minutes

Chicken and Sausage Fettuccine

1 (12-ounce) package BOB EVANS® Original Links
1 boneless, skinless chicken breast, thinly sliced
1 tablespoon olive oil
1 small zucchini, quartered and sliced
4 medium mushrooms, sliced
3 green onions, sliced
1 (12-ounce) package uncooked fettucine
½ cup butter or margarine
½ cup milk
¼ cup grated Parmesan cheese
1 teaspoon garlic powder
1 teaspoon hot pepper sauce
Salt and black pepper to taste

Cook sausage in large skillet until browned. Remove from skillet and cut into ½-inch slices. Add chicken to skillet; cook in sausage drippings until no longer pink. Remove and set aside. Heat olive oil in skillet; add zucchini, mushrooms and green onions and cook until crisp-tender. Cook fettucine in large saucepan according to package directions; drain and return to saucepan. Add butter and milk; toss gently until evenly coated. Add sausage, chicken, vegetable mixture, cheese, garlic powder and hot pepper sauce; cook over low heat, tossing gently until well blended and heated through. Add salt and black pepper to taste. Refrigerate leftovers.

Makes 6 servings

Mariachi Chicken

Fish with Hidden Valley Ranch® Tartar Sauce

    1 cup (½ pint) sour cream
    ¼ cup chopped sweet pickles
    1 packet (1 ounce) HIDDEN VALLEY® The Original Ranch® Salad Dressing & Seasoning Mix
    ¾ cup dry bread crumbs
  1½ pounds white fish fillets (sole, flounder, snapper or turbot)
    1 egg, beaten
      Vegetable oil
      French fried shoestring potatoes (optional)
      Lemon wedges (optional)

To make sauce, in small bowl, combine sour cream, pickles and 2 tablespoons of the salad dressing & seasoning mix; cover and refrigerate. On large plate, combine bread crumbs and remaining salad dressing mix. Dip fillets in egg, then coat with bread crumb mixture. Fry fillets in 3 tablespoons oil until golden. (Add more oil to pan if necessary to prevent sticking.) Serve with chilled sauce. Serve with lemon wedges, if desired. *Makes 4 servings*

Quick & Easy Broccoli Chicken

    1 (6.9-ounce) package RICE-A-RONI® Chicken Flavor
    2 tablespoons margarine or butter
    1 teaspoon dried basil
    4 boneless, skinless chicken breast halves (about 1 pound)
    2 cups broccoli flowerets
    1 tomato, chopped
    1 cup (4 ounces) shredded mozzarella or Cheddar cheese

1. In large skillet over medium heat, sauté rice-vermicelli mix with margarine until vermicelli is golden brown.

2. Slowly stir in 2 cups water, basil and Special Seasonings. Bring to a boil. Place chicken over rice. Reduce heat to low. Cover; simmer 10 minutes.

3. Stir in broccoli and tomato. Cover; simmer 10 minutes or until rice is tender and chicken is no longer pink inside. Sprinkle with cheese. Cover; let stand 3 minutes or until cheese is melted. *Makes 4 servings*

Tip: If you prefer, use green beans or whole-kernel corn instead of broccoli.

Fish with Hidden Valley Ranch® Tartar Sauce

Smoky Mountain Chicken and Rice Casserole

      Vegetable cooking spray
  2 cups sour cream
  1 (10¾-ounce) can condensed cream of chicken soup
  2 canned chipotle peppers in adobo sauce, finely chopped
  1 teaspoon salt
  1 teaspoon pepper
  3 cups cooked rice
  2 cups shredded cooked chicken
  2 cups shredded smoked Cheddar cheese

Preheat oven to 400°F. Lightly coat 13×9×2-inch baking dish with vegetable cooking spray. In large bowl, stir together sour cream, soup, chipotles, salt and pepper until well blended. Stir in rice, chicken and cheese. Spoon into baking dish. Bake uncovered in preheated oven 20 to 25 minutes, until edges of casserole are bubbly. Turn oven to broil setting and lightly brown casserole.   *Makes 8 to 10 servings*

Favorite recipe from **USA Rice**

Quick Mediterranean Fish

  1 medium onion, sliced
  2 tablespoons olive oil
  1 clove garlic, crushed
  1 can (14½ ounces) DEL MONTE® Stewed Tomatoes - Italian Recipe
  3 to 4 tablespoons medium salsa
  ¼ teaspoon ground cinnamon
  1½ pounds firm fish (such as halibut, red snapper or sea bass)
  12 stuffed green olives, halved crosswise

Microwave Directions

1. Combine onion, oil and garlic in 1½-quart microwavable dish. Cover and microwave on HIGH 3 minutes; drain.

2. Stir in tomatoes, salsa and cinnamon. Top with fish and olives.

3. Cover and microwave on HIGH 3 to 4 minutes or until fish flakes easily with fork. Garnish with chopped parsley, if desired.   *Makes 4 to 6 servings*

Smoky Mountain Chicken and Rice Casserole

Skillet Beef & Broccoli

    1 **tablespoon BERTOLLI® Olive Oil**
    1 **pound sirloin steak, cut into 1-inch strips**
    1 **package (10 ounces) frozen broccoli florets, thawed**
    1 **envelope LIPTON® RECIPE SECRETS® Onion Soup Mix***
1¼ **cups water**
    1 **tablespoon firmly packed brown sugar**
    1 **tablespoon soy sauce**

*Also terrific with LIPTON® RECIPE SECRETS® Onion Mushroom Soup Mix.

1. In 12-inch nonstick skillet, heat oil over medium-high heat and brown steak, stirring occasionally, in two batches. Remove steak from skillet and set aside.

2. Stir in broccoli and soup mix blended with water, brown sugar and soy sauce. Bring to a boil over high heat. Reduce heat to low and simmer uncovered, stirring occasionally, 2 minutes.

3. Return steak to skillet and cook 1 minute or until steak is done. Serve, if desired, with hot cooked rice. *Makes 4 servings*

Prep Time: 10 minutes
Cook Time: 15 minutes

Creamy Chicken Primavera

    1 **teaspoon olive oil**
    2 **medium red, yellow or green bell peppers, coarsely chopped**
    1 **medium onion, chopped**
    1 **pound boneless, skinless chicken breasts, cut into 1-inch pieces**
½ **cup frozen green peas, thawed**
    1 **jar (1 pound) RAGÚ® Cheesy!® Light Parmesan Alfredo Sauce**
⅛ **teaspoon ground black pepper**
    8 **ounces linguine or spaghetti, cooked and drained**

1. In 12-inch nonstick skillet, heat olive oil over medium-high heat and cook red bell peppers and onion, stirring occasionally, 10 minutes or until golden.

2. Stir in chicken and peas and continue cooking, stirring occasionally, 5 minutes. Stir in Ragú Cheesy! Sauce and black pepper.

3. Reduce heat to medium and simmer, stirring occasionally, 10 minutes or until chicken is thoroughly cooked. Serve over hot linguine. *Makes 4 servings*

Skillet Beef & Broccoli

Tortellini Bake Parmesano

1 package (12 ounces) fresh or frozen cheese tortellini or ravioli
½ pound lean ground beef
½ medium onion, finely chopped
2 cloves garlic, minced
½ teaspoon dried oregano, crushed
1 can (26 ounces) DEL MONTE® Chunky Spaghetti Sauce with Garlic & Herb
2 small zucchini, sliced
⅓ cup (about 1½ ounces) grated Parmesan cheese

1. Cook pasta according to package directions; rinse and drain.

2. Meanwhile, brown beef with onion, garlic and oregano in large skillet over medium-high heat; drain. Season with salt and pepper, if desired.

3. Add spaghetti sauce and zucchini. Cook 15 minutes or until thickened, stirring occasionally.

4. Arrange half of pasta in oiled 2-quart microwavable dish; top with half each of sauce and cheese. Repeat layers ending with cheese; cover.

5. Microwave on HIGH 8 to 10 minutes or until heated through, rotating dish halfway through cooking time.   *Makes 4 servings*

Hint: For convenience, double recipe and freeze one for later use. The recipe can also be made ahead, refrigerated and heated just before serving (allow extra time in microwave if dish is chilled).

Prep and Cook Time: **35 minutes**

Apple Curry Chicken

   4 boneless, skinless chicken breast halves
1½ teaspoons curry powder, divided
   ¼ teaspoon salt
   4 teaspoons vegetable oil, divided
   1 Golden Delicious apple, peeled, chopped
   ⅓ cup chopped onion
   ½ cup mango chutney, chopped
   ⅓ cup water
      Hot cooked couscous or rice (optional)

With meat mallet or similar utensil, pound chicken to ¼-inch thickness; sprinkle chicken with half of curry powder and salt. In nonstick skillet, place 2 teaspoons oil and heat to medium-high temperature. Add chicken and cook, turning, 8 to 10 minutes or until chicken is brown and fork tender. Remove chicken to platter; keep warm. To same skillet, add remaining 2 teaspoons oil and heat to medium-high temperature. Add apple and onion and cook, stirring, 2 to 3 minutes or until apple and onion are almost tender. Stir in chutney, water, and remaining curry; heat to boiling and boil 1 minute to thicken slightly. Spoon over chicken. Serve with couscous or rice.

Makes 4 servings

*Favorite recipe from **Delmarva Poultry Industry, Inc.***

Tuna-Stuffed Bakers

4 large baking potatoes or sweet potatoes, scrubbed
2 cups chopped or sliced, fresh or frozen vegetables*
¼ cup chopped green onions
1 (7-ounce) STARKIST Flavor Fresh Pouch® Tuna (Albacore or Chunk Light)
⅓ cup low-fat ricotta cheese
2 tablespoons drained pimiento strips
1 tablespoon chopped fresh parsley (optional)
¼ teaspoon dry mustard
⅛ teaspoon pepper
4 slices (1 ounce each) reduced-calorie American cheese, cut into ¼-inch strips

Suggested vegetables are: broccoli or cauliflower florets, mushrooms, carrots, pea pods, peas, asparagus or corn.

Microwave Directions

Pierce potatoes twice with fork. Arrange potatoes 1 inch apart on paper towel in microwave oven. Micro-cook on HIGH power for 10½ to 12½ minutes, turning and rearranging potatoes halfway through cooking time. Wrap potatoes in foil; let stand for 5 minutes to finish cooking while preparing filling.

For filling, in 2-quart microwavable casserole place desired vegetables and onions. Cover with waxed paper; micro-cook on HIGH power for 3 to 5 minutes, or until vegetables are crisp-tender, stirring twice. Drain. Stir in tuna, ricotta cheese, pimiento, parsley, mustard and pepper until well combined. Cover; micro-cook on HIGH power for 2 minutes, or until mixture is heated through, stirring once.

Unwrap potatoes; cut lengthwise into halves. Flake interior with fork. Spoon vegetable filling mixture over potatoes, mounding filling on top. Place potatoes in shallow microwavable dish. Place strips of cheese diagonally over filling. Micro-cook on HIGH power for 1 to 2 minutes, or until cheese is melted.

Makes 4 servings

Prep Time: 20 minutes

Tuna-Stuffed Bakers

Chuckwagon BBQ Rice Round-Up

    1 **pound lean ground beef**
    1 **(6.8-ounce) package RICE-A-RONI® Beef Flavor**
    2 **tablespoons margarine or butter**
    2 **cups frozen corn**
  ½ **cup prepared barbecue sauce**
  ½ **cup (2 ounces) shredded Cheddar cheese**

1. In large skillet over medium-high heat, brown ground beef until well cooked. Remove from skillet; drain. Set aside.

2. In same skillet over medium heat, sauté rice-vermicelli mix with margarine until vermicelli is golden brown.

3. Slowly stir in 2½ cups water, corn and Special Seasonings; bring to a boil. Reduce heat to low. Cover; simmer 15 to 20 minutes or until rice is tender.

4. Stir in barbecue sauce and ground beef. Sprinkle with cheese. Cover; let stand 3 to 5 minutes or until cheese is melted.   *Makes 4 servings*

Tip: Salsa can be substituted for barbecue sauce.

Teriyaki Steak with Onions and Mushrooms

    1 **boneless beef sirloin steak, about 1 inch thick (1½ pounds)**
  ¾ **cup light teriyaki sauce, divided**
    1 **tablespoon vegetable oil**
    1 **can (8 ounces) sliced mushrooms, drained**
    1 **small red or green bell pepper, cut into strips**
1⅓ **cups *French's*® French Fried Onions, divided**

1. Brush each side of steak with 1 tablespoon teriyaki sauce. Heat oil in grill pan or heavy skillet over medium-high heat. Cook steak for 3 to 4 minutes per side or until desired doneness. Remove steak; keep warm.

2. Add mushrooms and bell pepper to pan; cook until pepper is crisp-tender. Stir in remaining teriyaki sauce and ⅔ *cup* French Fried Onions; heat through.

3. Serve mushroom mixture over steak. Sprinkle with remaining onions.   *Makes 6 servings*

Chuckwagon BBQ Rice Round-Up

Chicken Marsala

  1 tablespoon butter
  4 boneless skinless chicken breasts (about 1 pound)
  1 cup sliced carrots
  1 cup sliced fresh mushrooms
  ⅓ cup chicken broth
  ⅓ cup HOLLAND HOUSE® Marsala Cooking Wine

Melt butter in skillet over medium-high heat. Add chicken; cook 5 minutes. Turn chicken over; add remaining ingredients. Bring to a boil; simmer 15 to 20 minutes until juices run clear. Serve over cooked fettuccine, if desired.

Makes 4 servings

San Marino Chicken

  1 chicken (3 pounds), skinned and cut up
  ¼ cup all-purpose flour
  1 can (8 ounces) tomato sauce
  ⅓ cup chopped sun-dried tomatoes, packed in oil
  ¼ cup red wine
  1 tablespoon grated lemon peel
  2 cups sliced mushrooms
  2 cups *French's*® French Fried Onions, divided
    Hot cooked rice or pasta (optional)

Slow Cooker Directions

1. Lightly coat chicken pieces with flour. Place chicken in slow cooker. Add tomato sauce, sun-dried tomatoes, wine and lemon peel. Cover and cook on LOW setting for 4 hours (or on HIGH for 2 hours).

2. Add mushrooms and *1 cup* French Fried Onions. Cover and cook on LOW setting for 2 hours (or on HIGH for 1 hour) until chicken is no longer pink near bone. Remove chicken to heated platter. Skim fat from sauce.

3. Serve chicken with hot cooked rice or pasta, if desired. Spoon sauce on top and sprinkle with remaining onions.

Makes 4 servings

Prep Time: 5 minutes
Cook Time: 6 hours

Chicken Marsala

Quick Beef Bourguignonne

  3 tablespoons all-purpose flour
½ teaspoon dried thyme
½ teaspoon ground black pepper
¾ pound boneless sirloin or top round steak, cut into 1-inch pieces
  2 tablespoons vegetable oil, divided
  3 cups (8 ounces) halved or quartered cremini or white mushrooms
⅓ cup thinly sliced shallots or chopped onion
  1 (14½-ounce) can beef broth
¼ cup water
¼ cup dry red wine or water
  1 (4.8-ounce) package PASTA RONI® Garlic Alfredo
¾ cup thinly sliced carrots

1. Combine flour, thyme and pepper in resealable plastic food storage bag. Add steak; shake to coat evenly with flour mixture.

2. In large skillet over medium-high heat, heat 1 tablespoon oil. Add steak; cook 3 minutes or until lightly browned on all sides. Remove from skillet; set aside.

3. In same skillet over medium heat, heat remaining 1 tablespoon oil. Add mushrooms and shallots; cook 3 minutes, stirring occasionally.

4. Add beef broth, ¼ cup water and wine; bring to a boil. Add pasta, steak, carrots and Special Seasonings. Reduce heat to medium. Simmer 5 minutes or until pasta is tender. Let stand 5 minutes before serving.

Makes 4 servings

Prep Time: 15 minutes
Cook Time: 20 minutes

Skillet Chicken, Mushrooms and Vegetables

    3 tablespoons bottled Italian dressing, divided
    1 pound boneless skinless chicken breasts
    1 pound fresh white mushrooms, sliced
    2 plum tomatoes, diced
    1 large carrot, cut in matchsticks or thinly sliced*
    3 green onions, sliced
      Steamed rice (optional)

For carrot matchsticks, cut carrot into thin diagonal slices; stack 3 or 4 slices and cut in narrow sticks.

Heat 1 tablespoon dressing in large nonstick skillet over medium-high heat. Add chicken; cook about 2 minutes or until browned. Remove and set aside. Add remaining 2 tablespoons dressing to same skillet. Add mushrooms; cook 4 minutes stirring frequently, until mushrooms begin to release their liquid. Stir in tomatoes, carrot and reserved chicken. Reduce heat; cover and simmer 10 minutes or until juices run clear when chicken is pierced with fork. Remove chicken and vegetables to heated platter. Cook sauce in skillet 2 minutes to thicken slightly; pour over chicken. Sprinkle with green onions. Serve with steamed rice, if desired.   *Makes 4 servings*

Favorite recipe from **Mushroom Information Center**

Rustic Dijon Chicken with Tomato Pesto

    1 tablespoon olive oil
    1 teaspoon minced garlic
    4 boneless skinless chicken breast halves (1 pound)
    1 can (14½ ounces) diced tomatoes or crushed tomatoes in purée, undrained
    1 container (4 ounces) prepared pesto sauce
 1⅓ cups *French's®* French Fried Onions, divided
    2 tablespoons *French's®* Honey Dijon Mustard
      Hot cooked noodles or pasta

1. Heat oil in 12-inch nonstick skillet over medium-high heat. Add garlic; sauté 30 seconds. Add chicken; sauté 5 minutes or until chicken is browned on both sides.

2. Add tomatoes with juice, pesto sauce, *1 cup* French Fried Onions and mustard. Reduce heat to medium-low. Simmer 5 minutes or until chicken is no longer pink in center and sauce thickens slightly.

3. To serve, arrange chicken over hot cooked noodles or pasta. Top with sauce and sprinkle with remaining onions.   *Makes 4 servings*

Skillet Chicken, Mushrooms and Vegetables

Lemon Catfish Bake

2 tablespoons butter or margarine, melted
2 tablespoons lemon juice
¼ cup dry bread crumbs
½ teaspoon LAWRY'S® Seasoned Salt
¾ teaspoon LAWRY'S® Lemon Pepper
¼ teaspoon dill weed
1 pound catfish fillets
  Paprika
4 lemon slices (garnish)

In shallow dish, combine butter and lemon juice; set aside. In another shallow dish, combine bread crumbs, Seasoned Salt, Lemon Pepper and dill weed. Pat fillets dry. Dip in butter mixture, then in bread crumb mixture. Place in ungreased 12×8×2-inch baking dish. Pour remaining butter mixture over fillets; sprinkle lightly with paprika. Bake, uncovered, in 350°F oven for 25 to 30 minutes or until fish begins to flake easily with fork. *Makes 4 servings*

Hint: Garnish with lemon slices, and serve with fresh steamed vegetables, potatoes or rice.

Variation: Any type of fish fillets may be substituted.

Prep Time: 10 minutes
Cook Time: 25 to 30 minutes

Simple Stir-Fry

1 tablespoon vegetable oil
12 boneless, skinless chicken breast tenderloins, cut into 1-inch pieces
1 bag (1 pound) frozen stir-fry vegetable mix
2 tablespoons soy sauce
2 tablespoons honey
2 (2-cup) bags UNCLE BEN'S® Boil-in-Bag Rice

1. Heat oil in large skillet or wok. Add chicken; cook over medium-high heat 6 to 8 minutes or until lightly browned. Add vegetables, soy sauce and honey. Cover and cook 5 to 8 minutes or until chicken is no longer pink in center and vegetables are crisp-tender.

2. Meanwhile, cook rice according to package directions. Serve stir-fry over rice.

Makes 4 servings

Lemon Catfish Bake

Creamy Chicken and Linguine

8 ounces linguine
¼ cup CRISCO® Canola Oil*
2 boneless chicken breast halves, cut into bite-size pieces
1 onion, finely chopped
2 cloves garlic, minced
8 ounces button mushrooms, sliced
½ teaspoon salt
⅛ teaspoon pepper
⅛ teaspoon cayenne pepper
3 green onions, thinly sliced
1 (15-ounce) can diced tomatoes
1 (5-ounce) can PET® Evaporated Milk

Or use your favorite Crisco Oil.

Cook linguine according to package directions; drain.

In a large skillet, heat CRISCO Oil over medium heat. Add chicken, onion, garlic, and mushrooms; sauté until onions are soft and chicken is lightly browned. Stir in salt, pepper, and cayenne pepper. Add green onions, diced tomatoes with juice and PET® Evaporated Milk; bring to a boil, reduce heat and stir. Simmer 5 to 6 minutes. Toss with pasta; serve.

Makes 4 to 6 servings

Prep Time: 10 minutes
Cook Time: 15 minutes

Ranch Baked Quesadillas

1 cup shredded cooked chicken
1 cup (4 ounces) shredded Monterey Jack cheese
½ cup HIDDEN VALLEY® The Original Ranch® Salad Dressing
¼ cup diced green chiles, rinsed and drained
4 (9-inch) flour tortillas, heated
Salsa and guacamole (optional)

Combine chicken, cheese, dressing and chiles in a medium bowl. Place about ½ cup chicken mixture on each tortilla; fold in half. Place quesadillas on a baking sheet. Bake at 350°F. for 15 minutes or until cheese is melted. Cut into thirds, if desired. Serve with salsa and guacamole, if desired.

Makes 4 servings

Family Favorites

There are some wonderful home-cooked dishes no one ever gets tired of. They're the kind of unpretentious food you just can't get at a restaurant (and even if you could it wouldn't taste as good). Dishes such as Tuna Noodle Casserole and Classic Fried Chicken are American comfort food at its finest. You'll find recipes here for the kind of warm family meals everyone, including picky eaters, will love. Who could resist Oven-Baked Stew or Cheeseburger Macaroni? Why would anyone want to?

Southwestern Chicken Taco Salad

Aluminum foil
Nonstick cooking spray
6 (8-inch) plain or flavored flour tortillas
2 (10-ounce) cans HORMEL® chunk breast of chicken, drained and flaked
1 tablespoon taco seasoning mix
2 tablespoons water
1 (15-ounce) can red kidney beans, drained and rinsed
1 (11-ounce) can whole kernel Mexican corn, drained
6 cups shredded lettuce
1 cup shredded cheddar cheese
1 tomato, diced
1 avocado, diced
1 cup salsa, drained
½ cup sour cream

Preheat oven to 350°F. Make six 2½-inch balls of foil by slightly crushing six 12×12-inch pieces of foil. Lightly spray one side of each flour tortilla and inside of 6 (10-ounce) custard or small baking dishes with nonstick cooking spray. Gently press tortillas, sprayed sides up, into custard cups; folding edges to fit as necessary. Place ball of foil in center of each cup. Place cups onto baking sheet. Bake shells 10 minutes, remove from oven and remove foil balls. Return to oven and continue baking an additional 3 to 5 minutes or until shells are crisp and edges are lightly browned. Meanwhile, in skillet, combine chunk chicken, taco seasoning mix and 2 tablespoons water. Simmer over low heat for 3 to 5 minutes. Add beans and corn. Heat until warmed through. Place 1 cup shredded lettuce into each tortilla shell. Fill with meat mixture. Top with cheese, tomato and avocado. In small bowl, combine salsa and sour cream. Drizzle dressing over salad and serve.

Makes 6 servings

Tuna Noodle Casserole

   1 can (10¾ ounces) condensed cream of mushroom soup
   1 cup milk
   3 cups hot cooked rotini pasta (2 cups uncooked)
   1 can (12½ ounces) tuna packed in water, drained and flaked
1⅓ cups *French's®* French Fried Onions, divided
   1 package (10 ounces) frozen peas and carrots
   ½ cup (2 ounces) shredded Cheddar or grated Parmesan cheese

Microwave Directions

Combine soup and milk in 2-quart microwavable shallow casserole. Stir in pasta, tuna, ⅔ *cup* French Fried Onions, vegetables and cheese. Cover; microwave on HIGH 10 minutes* or until heated through, stirring halfway through cooking time. Top with remaining ⅔ *cup* onions. Microwave 1 minute or until onions are golden.   *Makes 6 servings*

*Or bake, covered, in 350°F oven 25 to 30 minutes.

Tip: Garnish with chopped pimiento and parsley sprigs, if desired.

Prep Time: 10 minutes
Cook Time: 11 minutes

Yummy Weeknight Chicken

   1 pound boneless skinless chicken breasts, pounded thin
   1 small onion, sliced
   1 package (10 ounces) mushrooms, sliced
   ⅓ cup barbecue sauce
   ¼ cup honey
   2 tablespoons *French's®* Worcestershire Sauce

1. Heat *1 tablespoon oil* in large nonstick skillet over medium-high heat. Cook chicken 5 minutes until chicken is no longer pink in center. Remove chicken to serving platter; keep warm.

2. In same skillet, sauté onion and mushrooms for 5 minutes or until mushrooms are golden brown and no liquid remains. Return chicken to skillet.

3. Combine remaining ingredients. Pour into skillet. Bring to a full boil. Reduce heat and cook 2 to 3 minutes or until sauce thickens slightly, stirring occasionally. Serve with hot cooked rice, if desired.   *Makes 4 servings*

Prep Time: 10 minutes
Cook Time: 12 minutes

Tuna Noodle Casserole

Lemon Rosemary Roast Chicken

   1 whole chicken (about 4 to 4½ pounds)
  2½ teaspoons LAWRY'S® Seasoned Salt
   2 teaspoons whole dried rosemary, crumbled
   1 teaspoon LAWRY'S® Lemon Pepper

Rinse chicken with cold water; pat dry with paper towels. In small bowl, combine Seasoned Salt, rosemary and Lemon Pepper. Gently lift skin from meat on breast. Rub seasoning mixture onto meat under skin, all over outside of chicken and inside cavity. Place chicken, breast-side-up, in 13×9×2-inch baking dish. Roast in 400°F oven for 60 minutes or until meat thermometer inserted in thickest part of chicken thigh reaches 180°F. Let stand 10 minutes before carving.

Makes 8 servings

Hint: Loosely 'crunch up' some foil in the baking dish around the chicken to keep grease from splattering in the oven. Also, elevate the chicken on a cooling rack in the dish to help brown the bottom of chicken.

Prep Time: 10 minutes
Cook Time: 60 to 70 minutes

Meatball Bake

   1 jar (1 pound 10 ounces) RAGÚ® Chunky Pasta Sauce
   2 cups water
   2 cups uncooked instant rice
   1 cup frozen green peas, thawed
 1½ cups shredded mozzarella cheese (about 6 ounces)
   1 package (12 ounces) frozen fully cooked cocktail-size meatballs, thawed

Preheat oven to 375°F. Spray 13×9-inch glass baking dish with nonstick cooking spray; set aside.

In large bowl, combine Pasta Sauce, water, rice, peas, 1 cup cheese and meatballs. Spoon into prepared baking dish.

Bake, uncovered, 25 minutes. Sprinkle with remaining ½ cup cheese and bake an additional 5 minutes or until cheese is melted. Let stand 5 minutes before serving.

Makes 6 servings

Prep Time: 10 minutes
Cook Time: 30 minutes

Lemon Rosemary Roast Chicken

Rapid Ragú® Chili

1½ **pounds lean ground beef**
1 **medium onion, chopped**
2 **tablespoons chili powder**
1 **can (19 ounces) red kidney beans, rinsed and drained**
1 **jar (1 pound 10 ounces) RAGÚ® Old World Style® Pasta Sauce**
1 **cup shredded Cheddar cheese (about 4 ounces)**

1. In 12-inch skillet, brown ground beef with onion and chili powder over medium-high heat, stirring occasionally. Stir in beans and Ragú Pasta Sauce.

2. Bring to a boil over high heat. Reduce heat to low and simmer covered, stirring occasionally, 20 minutes. Top with cheese. Serve, if desired, over hot cooked rice.   *Makes 6 servings*

Prep Time: 10 minutes
Cook Time: 25 minutes

Oven-Baked Stew

2 **pounds boneless beef chuck or round steak, cut into 1-inch cubes**
¼ **cup all-purpose flour**
1⅓ **cups sliced carrots**
1 **can (14 to 16 ounces) whole peeled tomatoes, undrained and chopped**
1 **envelope LIPTON® RECIPE SECRETS® Onion Soup Mix***
½ **cup dry red wine or water**
1 **cup fresh or canned sliced mushrooms**
1 **package (8 ounces) medium or broad egg noodles, cooked and drained**

*Also terrific with LIPTON® RECIPE SECRETS® Beefy Onion, Onion Mushroom or Beefy Mushroom Soup Mix.

1. Preheat oven to 425°F. In 2½-quart shallow casserole, toss beef with flour, then bake uncovered 20 minutes, stirring once.

2. *Reduce heat to 350°F.* Stir in carrots, tomatoes, soup mix and wine.

3. Bake covered 1½ hours or until beef is tender. Stir in mushrooms and bake covered an additional 10 minutes. Serve over hot noodles.   *Makes 8 servings*

Slow Cooker Method: In slow cooker, toss beef with flour. Add carrots, tomatoes, soup mix and wine. Cook covered on LOW 8 to 10 hours. Add mushrooms; cook covered on LOW 30 minutes or until beef is tender. Serve over hot noodles.

Prep Time: 20 minutes
Cook Time: 2 hours

Rapid Ragú® Chili

Chicken Fried Rice

 1 bag SUCCESS® Rice
 ½ pound boneless skinless chicken, cut into ½-inch pieces
 ½ teaspoon salt
 ¼ teaspoon pepper
 2 tablespoons vegetable oil
 1 clove garlic, minced
 ½ teaspoon grated fresh ginger
 2 cups diagonally sliced green onions
 1 cup sliced fresh mushrooms
 2 tablespoons reduced-sodium soy sauce
 1 teaspoon sherry
 1 teaspoon Asian-style hot chili sesame oil (optional)

Prepare rice according to package directions.

Sprinkle chicken with salt and pepper; set aside. Heat oil in large skillet over medium-high heat. Add garlic and ginger; cook and stir 1 minute. Add chicken; stir-fry until no longer pink in center. Add green onions and mushrooms; stir-fry until tender. Stir in soy sauce, sherry and sesame oil. Add rice; heat thoroughly, stirring occasionally.   *Makes 6 servings*

Roasted Chicken & Garlic Provençale

 1 envelope LIPTON® RECIPE SECRETS® Savory Herb with Garlic Soup Mix
 3 tablespoons BERTOLLI® Olive Oil
 2 tablespoons water
 1 tablespoon white wine vinegar (optional)
 1 (2½- to 3-pound) chicken, cut into serving pieces
 1 large onion, cut into 8 wedges
 1 large tomato, cut into 8 wedges

1. Preheat oven to 425°F. In small bowl, blend soup mix, oil, water and vinegar.

2. In bottom of broiler pan without rack, arrange chicken, onion and tomato. Evenly pour soup mixture over chicken and vegetables.

3. Roast 45 minutes or until chicken is thoroughly cooked.   *Makes 4 servings*

Did you know? Recipes prepared in the style of Provence, a region in southeastern France, are typically prepared with garlic, tomatoes and olive oil. Other ingredients common to this region include onions, olives, mushrooms, anchovies and eggplant.

Chicken Fried Rice

Cheeseburger Macaroni

1 cup mostaccioli or elbow macaroni, uncooked
1 pound ground beef
1 medium onion, chopped
1 can (14½ ounces) DEL MONTE® Diced Tomatoes with Basil, Garlic & Oregano
¼ cup DEL MONTE® Tomato Ketchup
1 cup (4 ounces) shredded Cheddar cheese

1. Cook pasta according to package directions; drain.

2. Brown meat with onion in large skillet; drain. Season with salt and pepper, if desired. Stir in undrained tomatoes, ketchup and pasta; heat through.

3. Top with cheese. Garnish, if desired.   *Makes 4 servings*

Prep Time: 8 minutes
Cook Time: 15 minutes

Classic Fried Chicken

¾ cup PILLSBURY BEST® All-Purpose Flour
1 teaspoon salt
¼ teaspoon pepper
1 frying chicken (2½ to 3 pounds), cut up
½ cup CRISCO® Oil*

Use your favorite Crisco Oil.

1. Combine flour, salt and pepper in paper or plastic bag. Add a few pieces of chicken at a time. Shake to coat.

2. Heat oil to 365°F in electric skillet or on medium-high heat in large heavy skillet. Fry chicken 30 to 40 minutes without lowering heat until no longer pink in center. Turn once for even browning. Drain on paper towels.   *Makes 4 servings*

Note: For thicker crust, increase flour to 1½ cups. Shake damp chicken in seasoned flour. Place on waxed paper. Let stand for 5 to 20 minutes before frying.

Spicy Fried Chicken: Increase pepper to ½ teaspoon. Combine pepper with ½ teaspoon poultry seasoning, ½ teaspoon paprika, ½ teaspoon cayenne pepper and ¼ teaspoon dry mustard. Rub on chicken before step 1. Substitute 2¼ teaspoons garlic salt, ¼ teaspoon salt and ¼ teaspoon celery salt for 1 teaspoon salt. Combine with flour in step 1 and proceed as directed above.

Cheeseburger Macaroni

Chicken Parmesan Pasta Toss

1 jar (1 pound 10 ounces) RAGÚ® Organic Pasta Sauce
8 ounces fusilli, bucati or your favorite pasta, cooked and drained
1 package (12 ounces) baked breaded low fat chicken breast tenders, heated according to package directions
2 cups shredded mozzarella cheese (about 8 ounces)

In 2-quart saucepan, heat Pasta Sauce.

In large serving bowl, combine hot Sauce, pasta, chicken and 1 cup cheese. Top with remaining 1 cup cheese and serve immediately. *Makes 4 servings*

Prep Time: 20 minutes

Chicken and Black Bean Enchiladas

2 jars (16 ounces each) mild picante sauce
¼ cup chopped fresh cilantro
2 tablespoons chili powder
1 teaspoon ground cumin
2 cups (10 ounces) chopped cooked chicken
1 can (15 ounces) black beans, drained and rinsed
1⅓ cups *French's®* French Fried Onions, divided
1 package (about 10 ounces) flour tortillas (7 inches)
1 cup (4 ounces) shredded Monterey Jack cheese with jalapeño peppers

Preheat oven to 350°F. Grease 15×10-inch jelly-roll baking pan. Combine picante sauce, cilantro, chili powder and cumin in large saucepan. Bring to a boil. Reduce heat to low; simmer 5 minutes.

Combine 1½ cups sauce mixture, chicken, beans and ⅔ *cup* French Fried Onions in medium bowl. Spoon a scant ½ cup filling over bottom third of each tortilla. Roll up tortillas enclosing filling and arrange, seam-side down, in a single layer in bottom of prepared baking pan. Spoon remaining sauce evenly over tortillas.

Bake, uncovered, 20 minutes or until heated through. Sprinkle with remaining ⅔ *cup* onions and cheese. Bake 5 minutes or until cheese is melted and onions are golden. Serve immediately.
Makes 5 to 6 servings (4 cups sauce, 4½ cups filling)

Tip: This is a great make-ahead party dish.

Prep Time: 45 minutes
Cook Time: 25 minutes

Chicken Parmesan Pasta Toss

Crunchy Fish Sticks with Rainbow Parmesan Pasta

⅔ cup milk
2 tablespoons margarine or butter
1 (5.1-ounce) package PASTA RONI® Angel Hair Pasta with Parmesan Cheese
2 cups frozen mixed vegetables or frozen chopped broccoli
  Crunchy Fish Sticks (recipe follows)

1. In large saucepan, bring 1⅓ cups water, milk and margarine to a boil.

2. Stir in pasta, vegetables and Special Seasonings; bring back to a boil. Reduce heat to medium. Gently boil uncovered, 4 to 5 minutes or until pasta is tender. Let stand 3 minutes before serving. Serve with Crunchy Fish Sticks or prepared frozen fish sticks.   *Makes 4 servings*

Prep Time: 20 minutes
Cook Time: 15 minutes

Crunchy Fish Sticks

3 tablespoons all-purpose flour
½ teaspoon ground black pepper
1 large egg
2 tablespoons milk
3 cups cornflakes, coarsely crushed
1 pound cod fillets, cut into 3×1-inch strips and patted dry
½ to ¾ cup vegetable oil

1. In shallow bowl, combine flour and pepper; set aside. In small bowl, combine egg and milk; set aside. In another shallow bowl, place crushed cornflakes; set aside.

2. Coat fish in flour mixture, dip in egg mixture, then roll in cornflakes, pressing coating gently on each fish strip.

3. In large skillet over medium heat, heat oil. Add fish strips; cook 3 to 4 minutes on each side or until golden brown and fish is cooked through. Drain.   *Makes 4 servings*

Crunchy Fish Sticks with Rainbow Parmesan Pasta

Apple Pecan Chicken Roll-Ups

½ **cup apple juice**
½ **cup UNCLE BEN'S® Instant Brown Rice**
½ **cup finely chopped unpeeled apple**
¼ **cup chopped pecans**
3 **tablespoons sliced green onions**
4 **boneless, skinless chicken breasts (about 1 pound)**
1 **tablespoon vegetable oil**

1. Heat oven to 400°F. In small saucepan, bring apple juice to a boil. Add rice, cover, reduce heat and simmer 8 to 10 minutes or until liquid is absorbed. Stir in apple, pecans and green onions. Remove from heat.

2. Flatten each chicken breast to about ¼-inch thickness by pounding between two pieces of waxed paper. Place ¼ of rice mixture on each chicken breast. Roll up, tucking in edges. Secure with toothpicks.

3. Heat oil in medium skillet over medium-high heat. Add chicken and cook 4 to 5 minutes or until lightly browned; place in shallow baking pan. Bake 20 to 25 minutes or until chicken is no longer pink in center.

Makes 4 servings

Cook's Tip: For this recipe, choose an apple variety that will retain its shape when cooked, such as Granny Smith, Golden Delicious or Jonathan.

Apple Pecan Chicken Roll-Up

Catfish with Tropical Fruit Salsa

　1 can (15.25 ounces) DOLE® Tropical Fruit Salad, drained
　1 can (8 ounces) low-sodium whole kernel corn, drained
　¼ cup chopped green onions
　2 tablespoons diced mild green chilies
　1 tablespoon chopped fresh cilantro or parsley
　1 pound catfish or red snapper fillets
　　Vegetable cooking spray
　2 tablespoons lime juice
　½ teaspoon paprika

• Chop tropical fruit salad. For salsa, stir together fruit salad, corn, onions, chilies and cilantro in small bowl. Set aside.

• Arrange fish in single layer on broiler pan sprayed with vegetable cooking spray.

• Broil 4 minutes; turn fish over. Brush with lime juice; sprinkle with paprika. Broil 3 to 5 minutes more or until fish flakes easily with fork. Remove fish to serving platter. Serve with tropical fruit salsa. Garnish with fresh cilantro sprigs and lime wedges, if desired.

Makes 4 servings

Prep Time: 10 minutes
Broil Time: 10 minutes

Mexican Pepper Steak

　1 cup WISH-BONE® Italian Dressing*
　1 cup salsa
　3 medium red, green and/or yellow bell peppers, quartered
　1 small red onion, cut into thick rings
　1½ pounds boneless sirloin or top loin steak, about 2 inches thick

*Also terrific with WISH-BONE® Robusto Italian or Just 2 Good! Italian Dressing.

In large, shallow nonaluminum baking dish or plastic bag, combine all ingredients except steak. Add steak; turn to coat. Cover, or close bag, and marinate in refrigerator, turning occasionally, 3 to 24 hours.

Remove steak and vegetables, reserving marinade. Grill or broil steak and vegetables, turning steak and vegetables once, until steak is done. Meanwhile, in small saucepan, bring reserved marinade to a boil and continue boiling 1 minute. Serve with steak and vegetables.

Makes 6 servings

Catfish with Tropical Fruit Salsa

One-Crust Chicken Pot Pie

⅓ CRISCO® Butter Flavor Stick or ⅓ cup CRISCO® Butter Flavor Shortening
⅓ cup chopped onion
½ cup all-purpose baking mix
½ teaspoon salt
¼ teaspoon pepper
⅛ teaspoon thyme
1½ cups chicken broth (homemade or canned)
⅔ cup milk (add 4 tablespoons PET® Evaporated Milk for a richer taste)
1½ cups frozen mixed vegetables
1¾ cups cooked chicken or turkey, chopped

Crust
2 cups all-purpose baking mix
4 tablespoons warm water
¼ CRISCO® Butter Flavor Stick or ¼ cup CRISCO® Butter Flavor Shortening

Preheat oven to 425°F. In a 2-quart saucepan, melt CRISCO Shortening; add onion and cook until translucent. Add all-purpose baking mix. Add salt, pepper and thyme, stirring constantly. Add broth, then milk; bring to a slow, low boil. Add vegetables and chicken; keep over low heat while preparing crust.

For crust, mix all-purpose baking mix with water and CRISCO Shortening. Pat out dough onto waxed paper; roll the crust to fit the dish you are using. The crust should be fairly thick. Carefully pour the filling into the baking dish. Fit the crust on top of the mixture; make slits for steam to escape. Bake for 25 to 30 minutes or until crust is lightly browned. *Makes 4 to 6 servings*

Prep Time: 25 minutes
Cook Time: 25 to 30 minutes

One-Crust Chicken Pot Pie

Lit'l Smokies 'n' Macaroni 'n' Cheese

1 package (7¼ ounces) macaroni and cheese mix, prepared according to package directions
1 pound HILLSHIRE FARM® Lit'l Smokies
1 can (10¾ ounces) condensed cream of celery or mushroom soup, undiluted
⅓ cup milk
1 tablespoon minced parsley (optional)
1 cup (4 ounces) shredded Cheddar cheese

Preheat oven to 350°F.

Combine prepared macaroni and cheese, Lit'l Smokies, soup, milk and parsley, if desired, in medium bowl. Pour into small greased casserole. Sprinkle Cheddar cheese over top. Bake, uncovered, 20 minutes or until heated through.   *Makes 8 servings*

Salmon with Citrus-Tomato Salsa

4 salmon fillets (about 1½ pounds)
4 tablespoons I CAN'T BELIEVE IT'S NOT BUTTER!® Spread, melted and divided
2 cans (14½ ounces each) diced tomatoes, drained
2 large navel oranges, peeled, sectioned and coarsely chopped
⅔ cup finely sliced green onions
⅓ cup chopped fresh cilantro
2 teaspoons finely chopped, seeded jalapeño pepper (optional)

Preheat oven to 400°F.

In 13×9-inch glass baking dish, arrange salmon. Brush with 2 tablespoons I Can't Believe It's Not Butter! Spread and season, if desired, with salt and ground black pepper; set aside.

In large bowl, combine remaining 2 tablespoons I Can't Believe It's Not Butter!® Spread, tomatoes, oranges, green onions, cilantro and jalapeño pepper. Season, if desired, with salt and ground black pepper; spoon over salmon.

Bake 25 minutes or until salmon is opaque and salsa is heated through.   *Makes 4 servings*

Note: Recipe can be halved.

Lit'l Smokies 'n' Macaroni 'n' Cheese

Spicy Buttermilk-Battered Fried Chicken

2 cups buttermilk
3 teaspoons red pepper sauce
1 3 to 4 pound chicken cut into 8 pieces, rinsed and patted dry
2½ cups PILLSBURY BEST® All-Purpose or Unbleached Flour
1 tablespoon dried oregano
1 tablespoon garlic powder
1 teaspoon paprika
1 teaspoon cayenne pepper
1 tablespoon salt
1 teaspoon freshly ground pepper
CRISCO® Canola Oil* as needed for frying

*Or use your favorite Crisco Oil.

In a shallow baking dish, whisk together the buttermilk and red pepper sauce. Add chicken pieces and turn to coat. Cover and refrigerate for a minimum of 2 hours and up to 24.

In a shallow baking dish, whisk together the PILLSBURY BEST® Flour, oregano, garlic powder, paprika, cayenne pepper, salt and freshly ground pepper. Toss the chicken pieces in the seasoned flour, a few at a time, until well coated. Dip chicken in the buttermilk mixture, then coat again in flour mixture.

In a large heavy skillet, pour CRISCO Oil to a depth of 1 inch. Heat the oil to 350°F. (Use a deep fryer thermometer to measure the temperature.)

Carefully add chicken pieces in a single layer, skin side down. Fry about 4 minutes; turn over and fry the other side for about 4 minutes. Turn again, frying a total of about 15 minutes, or until chicken is evenly golden brown, crisp and cooked through (170°F breast meat; 180°F dark meat).

Carefully remove cooked chicken from pan. Place on a paper towel-lined plate to drain. Serve warm or at room temperature.

Makes 4 servings

Note: For Extra-Hot Chicken, add an additional tablespoon of cayenne pepper to the flour-spice mixture.

Prep Time: 15 minutes
Cook Time: 30 minutes
Marinate Time: 2 to 24 hours

Spicy Buttermilk-Battered Fried Chicken

California Turkey Burgers

   1 pound ground turkey
   ½ cup finely chopped cilantro
   ⅓ cup plain dry bread crumbs
   1 egg, beaten
   3 tablespoons *French's*® Classic Yellow® Mustard
   ½ teaspoon salt
   ¼ teaspoon black pepper
   8 thin slices (3 ounces) Monterey Jack cheese
   ½ red or yellow bell pepper, seeded and cut into rings
   4 hamburger buns

1. Combine turkey, cilantro, bread crumbs, egg, mustard, salt and pepper in large bowl. Shape into 4 patties, pressing firmly.

2. Place patties on oiled grid. Grill over high heat 15 minutes or until no longer pink in center (165°F). Top burgers with cheese during last few minutes of grilling. Grill pepper rings 2 minutes. To serve, place burgers on buns and top with pepper rings. Serve with additional mustard, if desired.

Makes 4 servings

Prep Time: 15 minutes
Cook Time: 15 minutes

Hidden Valley® Broiled Fish

   1 packet (1 ounce) HIDDEN VALLEY® The Original Ranch® Salad Dressing & Seasoning Mix
   ⅓ cup lemon juice
   3 tablespoons olive oil
   3 tablespoons dry white wine or water
   1½ to 2 pounds mild white fish fillets, such as red snapper or sole

Combine salad dressing & seasoning mix, lemon juice, olive oil and wine in a shallow dish; mix well. Add fish and coat all sides with mixture. Cover and refrigerate for 15 to 30 minutes. Remove fish from marinade and place on broiler pan. Broil 9 to 12 minutes or until fish begins to flake when tested with a fork.

Makes 4 servings

California Turkey Burger

Hearty Entrées

Nothing satisfies like home-cooked pot roast, turkey breast or stuffed pork chops. These recipes will leave everyone from the hungriest teenager to the crankiest adult happy and contented. Enjoy the Cavemen Beef Back Ribs pictured here, or serve up Country Sausage with Macaroni and Cheese to please a crowd. Every dish is kitchen-tested and all the ingredients you need are available at the supermarket. The only thing better than sharing a delicious meal is enjoying the warmth and conversation that go with it.

Cavemen Beef Back Ribs
(page 188)

Hearty Shepherd's Pie

1½ **pounds ground beef**
2 **cups** *French's*® **French Fried Onions**
1 **can (10¾ ounces) condensed tomato soup**
2 **teaspoons Italian seasoning**
1 **package (10 ounces) frozen mixed vegetables, thawed**
3 **cups hot mashed potatoes**

1. Preheat oven to 375°F. Cook meat in large oven-proof skillet until browned; drain. Stir in *1 cup* French Fried Onions, soup, *½ cup water,* seasoning and ¼ *teaspoon each salt and pepper.*

2. Spoon vegetables over beef mixture. Top with mashed potatoes.

3. Bake 20 minutes or until hot. Sprinkle with remaining *1 cup* onions. Bake 2 minutes or until golden.   *Makes 6 servings*

Prep Time: 10 minutes
Cook Time: 27 minutes

Philly Cheesesteak Sandwiches

1 **box (1 pound 5 ounces) frozen thin beef sandwich steaks**
1 **tablespoon olive oil**
2 **large sweet onions, halved and thinly sliced**
1 **large red bell pepper, cut into ¼-inch strips**
¼ **teaspoon salt**
⅛ **teaspoon ground black pepper**
1 **jar (1 pound) RAGÚ® Cheesy! Double Cheddar Sauce**
4 **hoagie rolls, split**

In 12-inch nonstick skillet, cook steaks, 2 at a time, over medium-high heat, stirring occasionally and breaking into pieces, 2 minutes or until done. Remove from skillet; set aside and keep warm. Repeat with remaining steaks. Clean skillet.

In same skillet, heat olive oil over medium heat and cook onions and red pepper, stirring occasionally, 15 minutes or until onions are caramelized. Season with salt and pepper.

Return steaks to skillet with ½ of the Double Cheddar Sauce. Cook, stirring occasionally, 2 minutes or until heated through. To serve, evenly divide steak mixture on rolls, then drizzle with remaining Double Cheddar Sauce, heated.   *Makes 4 servings*

Prep Time: 10 minutes
Cook Time: 25 minutes

Hearty Shepherd's Pie

Classic Corned Beef Dinner

1 corned beef brisket (about 5 pounds)
2 medium onions, peeled and quartered
4 peppercorns
1 bay leaf
½ teaspoon dried rosemary leaves
1 quart (4 cups) water
6 medium potatoes (about 2 pounds), peeled and quartered
6 medium carrots, peeled and cut into 2-inch pieces
1 cup celery, cut into 2-inch pieces
1 medium head green cabbage, cut into wedges

Horseradish Sauce
2 tablespoons CRISCO® Stick or 2 tablespoons CRISCO® Shortening
2 tablespoons PILLSBURY BEST® All-Purpose Flour
½ teaspoon salt
⅛ teaspoon black pepper
1 egg yolk
1 cup milk
2 teaspoons prepared horseradish, or to taste
1 tablespoon lemon juice

1. Place beef in large Dutch oven with tight-fitting lid. Add onions, peppercorns, bay leaf, rosemary and water. Bring to a boil; simmer covered for 3½ hours or until meat is fork-tender.

2. Add potatoes, carrots and celery to Dutch oven. Place cabbage on top of meat. Cover and cook for 1 hour or until tender.

3. Meanwhile for Horseradish Sauce, melt CRISCO Shortening in saucepan over medium heat. Stir in flour, salt and pepper. Mix well and cook until bubbly, about 1 minute. Remove from heat. Beat egg yolk; add milk and mix well. Stir into CRISCO Shortening mixture. Cook over medium heat, stirring constantly, for 3 minutes or until smooth and thickened. Remove from heat. Stir in horseradish and lemon juice.

4. Remove vegetables and meat to large platter. Serve with Horseradish Sauce.

Makes 12 servings

Classic Corned Beef Dinner

French Bistro Ham

2 pounds sliced HILLSHIRE FARM® Ham

Dijon Glaze
¼ cup juices from cooked HILLSHIRE FARM® Ham
2 tablespoons Dijon mustard
2 tablespoons butter or margarine

Parsley Potatoes
1 pound small new potatoes
3 tablespoons butter
¼ cup chopped parsley
1 teaspoon salt
¼ teaspoon black pepper

Sauerkraut
1 pound sauerkraut
8 juniper berries, crushed (optional)

Prepare Ham according to directions on package. Reserve juices from cooked ham; set aside for Dijon Glaze.

For Dijon Glaze, mix reserved cooking juices and mustard in small bowl. Stir in butter and allow to melt.

For Parsley Potatoes, bring 4 quarts water to a boil in large saucepan over high heat. Boil potatoes until tender, about 20 minutes; drain. Melt butter in large skillet; add potatoes, parsley, salt and pepper, shaking skillet to coat potatoes.

For Sauerkraut, drain sauerkraut of most of its juices. Place in small saucepan with juniper berries, if desired. Heat gently over low heat about 7 minutes or until warmed through.

Serve Dijon Glaze over ham. Serve Parsley Potatoes and Sauerkraut alongside ham.

Makes 6 servings

Bistro Chicken Skillet

1 (2- to 2½-pound) whole chicken, cut into 8 pieces
2 teaspoons dried thyme
1 teaspoon paprika
1 teaspoon salt
½ teaspoon ground black pepper
2 tablespoons olive oil
8 large whole cloves garlic, peeled
¼ cup dry vermouth or water
2 tablespoons margarine or butter
1 (4.6-ounce) package PASTA RONI® Garlic & Olive Oil with Vermicelli
1½ cups fresh asparagus, cut into 1½-inch pieces, or broccoli florets
1 cup sliced carrots

1. Sprinkle meaty side of chicken with thyme, paprika, salt and pepper. In large skillet over medium-high heat, heat oil. Add chicken, seasoned-side down. Cook 5 minutes. Reduce heat to medium-low; turn chicken over. Add garlic. Cover; cook 20 to 25 minutes or until chicken is no longer pink inside.

2. Meanwhile, in medium saucepan, bring 1½ cups water, vermouth and margarine just to a boil. Stir in pasta, asparagus, carrots and Special Seasonings. Reduce heat to medium. Gently boil uncovered, 10 minutes or until pasta is tender, stirring occasionally.

3. Remove chicken and garlic from skillet with slotted spoon. Skim off and discard fat from skillet juices. Serve chicken, garlic and reserved juices over pasta.   *Makes 4 servings*

Prep Time: 10 minutes
Cook Time: 30 minutes

Bistro Chicken Skillet

Choucroute Garni

½ pound bacon, diced
2 large onions, peeled and coarsely chopped
3 carrots, pared and sliced
½ cup chopped parsley
2 bay leaves
10 black peppercorns
10 juniper berries
4 whole cloves
4 to 6 pounds refrigerated sauerkraut, rinsed well and drained
2 to 4 cups fruity white wine (like Riesling)
3 to 4 cups chicken broth
1 pound lean pork loin, cubed
½ pound ham, cubed
1 pound smoked sausage, sliced
1 pound bratwurst, sliced
2 tart green apples, cored and coarsely chopped

In a large Dutch oven, over medium-low heat, render bacon fat; add onion and carrots and sauté slowly; stirring occasionally, about 8 to 10 minutes. Place parsley, bay leaves, peppercorns, juniper berries and cloves in cheesecloth bag or large tea strainer. Add to pot along with sauerkraut, wine and broth. Bring to a boil; cover and simmer for 1 hour. Add meats to pot, stir, cover and simmer another hour. Add apples and simmer an additional 20 minutes. Serve immediately with pumpernickel or Jewish rye bread. Or refrigerate overnight and reheat to serve.

Makes 10 servings

Prep Time: 20 minutes
Cook Time: 140 minutes

*Favorite recipe from **National Pork Board***

Smothered Mexican Pork Chops

1 tablespoon vegetable oil
4 boneless thin-cut pork chops (about ¾ pound)
1 can (14½ ounces) chunky tomatoes, salsa- or Cajun-style
1 can (16 ounces) black beans, drained
2 cups BIRDS EYE® frozen Broccoli, Corn and Red Peppers*

Or, substitute 2 cups Birds Eye® frozen Corn.

• Heat oil in large skillet over high heat. Add pork; cook until browned, about 4 minutes per side.

• Add tomatoes; reduce heat to medium. Cover and cook 5 minutes. Uncover and push pork to side of skillet.

• Add beans and vegetables. Place pork on top of vegetables. Increase heat to medium-high; cover and cook 5 minutes or until heated through.   *Makes about 4 servings*

Prep Time: 5 minutes
Cook Time: 20 minutes

Harvest Pot Roast with Sweet Potatoes

1 envelope LIPTON® RECIPE SECRETS® Onion Soup Mix
1½ cups water
¼ cup soy sauce
2 tablespoons firmly packed dark brown sugar
1 teaspoon ground ginger (optional)
1 (3- to 3½-pound) boneless pot roast (rump, chuck or round)
4 large sweet potatoes, peeled, if desired, and cut into large chunks
3 tablespoons water
2 tablespoons all-purpose flour

1. Preheat oven to 325°F. In Dutch oven or 5-quart heavy ovenproof saucepot, combine soup mix, water, soy sauce, brown sugar and ginger; add roast.

2. Cover and bake 1 hour 45 minutes.

3. Add potatoes and bake covered an additional 45 minutes or until beef and potatoes are tender.

4. Remove roast and potatoes to serving platter and keep warm; reserve juices.

5. In small cup, with wire whisk, blend water and flour. In same Dutch oven, add flour mixture to reserved juices. Bring to a boil over high heat. Boil, stirring occasionally, 2 minutes. Serve with roast and potatoes.   *Makes 6 servings*

Smothered Mexican Pork Chop

Zesty Steak Fajitas

¾ cup *French's* Worcestershire Sauce, divided
1 pound boneless top round, sirloin or flank steak
3 tablespoons taco seasoning mix
2 red or green bell peppers, cut into quarters
1 to 2 large onions, cut into thick slices
¾ cup chili sauce
8 (8-inch) flour or corn tortillas, heated
   Sour cream and shredded cheese (optional)

1. Pour ½ cup Worcestershire over steak in deep dish. Cover and refrigerate 30 minutes or up to 3 hours. Drain meat and rub both sides with seasoning mix. Discard marinade.

2. Grill meat and vegetables over medium-hot coals 10 to 15 minutes until meat is medium rare and vegetables are charred, but tender.

3. Thinly slice meat and vegetables. Place in large bowl. Add chili sauce and ¼ cup Worcestershire. Toss to coat. Serve in tortillas and garnish with sour cream and cheese.

Makes 4 servings

Prep Time: 5 minutes
Cook Time: 15 minutes
Marinate Time: 30 minutes

Roast Beef with Red Wine Gravy

2 tablespoons oil
1 sirloin tip roast (3 to 4 pounds)
   Salt and black pepper
2 tablespoons all-purpose flour
1 jar (7 ounces) cocktail onions, drained
1 can (14½ ounces) beef broth
2 tablespoons HOLLAND HOUSE® Red Cooking Wine

Heat oven to 350°F. Heat oil in Dutch oven. Season roast to taste with salt and pepper; brown on all sides. Remove from Dutch oven. Drain excess fat, reserving ¼ cup drippings in Dutch oven. Sprinkle flour over reserved drippings. Cook over medium heat until lightly browned, stirring constantly. Add roast and onions to Dutch oven. Roast for 1¾ to 2¼ hours or until desired doneness. Remove roast to cutting board. Let stand 5 to 10 minutes before slicing. Gradually stir in beef broth and cooking wine in Dutch oven. Bring to a boil; reduce heat. Cook until gravy thickens. Slice roast and arrange with onions on serving platter. Serve with gravy.

Makes 6 servings

Zesty Steak Fajitas

Chicken and Linguine in Creamy Tomato Sauce

1 tablespoon olive oil
1 pound boneless, skinless chicken breasts, cut into ½-inch strips
1 jar (1 pound 10 ounces) RAGÚ® Old World Style® Pasta Sauce
2 cups water
8 ounces linguine or spaghetti
½ cup whipping or heavy cream
1 tablespoon chopped fresh basil leaves *or* ½ teaspoon dried basil leaves, crushed

1. In 12-inch skillet, heat olive oil over medium heat and brown chicken. Remove chicken and set aside.

2. In same skillet, stir in Ragú Pasta Sauce and water. Bring to a boil over high heat. Stir in uncooked linguine and return to a boil. Reduce heat to low and simmer covered, stirring occasionally, 15 minutes or until linguine is tender.

3. Stir in cream and basil. Return chicken to skillet and cook 5 minutes or until chicken is thoroughly cooked. *Makes 4 servings*

Buffalo-Style Skillet Steak

1¼ pounds boneless sirloin steak (1 inch thick)
4 tablespoons *Frank's® RedHot®* Original Cayenne Pepper Sauce, divided
Garlic powder and celery salt to taste
½ pound sliced fresh mushrooms
2 tablespoons crumbled blue cheese

1. Cut steak crosswise into 4 servings. Brush each lightly with *1 tablespoon **Frank's RedHot*** Sauce on both sides. Sprinkle with garlic powder and celery salt. Cover; let stand in refrigerator 15 minutes or longer, if desired.

2. Melt *1 tablespoon butter or margarine* in large skillet over medium-high heat. Add mushrooms and cook, stirring, until browned. Divide among 4 dinner plates; keep warm.

3. In same skillet, melt *1 tablespoon butter or margarine* over high heat. Cook steaks 1 minute per side. Reduce heat to medium and cook 3 minutes per side for medium-rare, or to desired doneness. Pour remaining *3 tablespoons **Frank's RedHot*** Sauce over steaks; turn to coat. Sprinkle with blue cheese. Serve on top of mushrooms. Pour any pan juices on top. *Makes 4 servings*

Chicken and Linguine in Creamy Tomato Sauce

Country Sausage Macaroni and Cheese

  1 pound BOB EVANS® Special Seasonings Roll Sausage
1½ cups milk
 12 ounces pasteurized processed Cheddar cheese, cut into cubes
 ½ cup Dijon mustard
  1 cup diced fresh or drained canned tomatoes
  1 cup sliced mushrooms
 ⅓ cup sliced green onions
 ⅛ teaspoon cayenne pepper
 12 ounces uncooked elbow macaroni
  2 tablespoons grated Parmesan cheese

Preheat oven to 350°F. Crumble and cook sausage in medium skillet until browned. Drain on paper towels. Combine milk, processed cheese and mustard in medium saucepan; cook and stir over low heat until cheese melts and mixture is smooth. Stir in sausage, tomatoes, mushrooms, green onions and cayenne pepper. Remove from heat.

Cook macaroni according to package directions; drain. Combine hot macaroni and cheese mixture in large bowl; toss until well coated. Spoon into greased shallow 2-quart casserole dish. Cover and bake 15 to 20 minutes. Stir; sprinkle with Parmesan cheese. Bake, uncovered, 5 minutes more. Let stand 10 minutes before serving. Refrigerate leftovers. *Makes 6 to 8 servings*

Skillet Chicken Alfredo

  4 boneless, skinless chicken breast halves (about 1¼ pounds)
  1 egg, lightly beaten
 ½ cup Italian seasoned dry bread crumbs
  2 tablespoons olive oil
  1 jar (1 pound) RAGÚ® Cheesy! Classic Alfredo Sauce
  1 small tomato, cut into 4 slices
  4 slices mozzarella cheese or ½ cup shredded mozzarella cheese (about 2 ounces)

1. Dip chicken in egg, then bread crumbs. In 12-inch nonstick skillet, heat olive oil over medium-high heat and lightly brown chicken. Remove chicken and set aside.

2. In same skillet, stir in Alfredo Sauce and bring to a boil. Reduce heat to low. Return chicken to skillet; arrange 1 tomato slice on each chicken breast half. Cover and simmer 5 minutes.

3. Evenly top chicken with cheese and simmer covered an additional 2 minutes or until chicken is thoroughly cooked. Serve, if desired, over hot cooked pasta and garnish with chopped fresh basil or parsley. *Makes 4 servings*

Country Sausage Macaroni and Cheese

Zesty Italian Stuffed Peppers

   3 **bell peppers (green, red or yellow)**
   1 **pound ground beef**
   1 **jar (14 ounces) spaghetti sauce**
1⅓ **cups** *French's*® **French Fried Onions, divided**
   2 **tablespoons** *Frank's*® *RedHot*® **Original Cayenne Pepper Sauce**
  ½ **cup uncooked instant rice**
  ¼ **cup sliced ripe olives**
   1 **cup (4 ounces) shredded mozzarella cheese**

Preheat oven to 400°F. Cut bell peppers in half lengthwise through stems; discard seeds. Place pepper halves, cut sides up, in shallow 2-quart baking dish; set aside.

Place beef in large microwavable bowl. Microwave on HIGH 5 minutes or until meat is browned, stirring once. Drain. Stir in spaghetti sauce, ⅔ *cup* French Fried Onions, *Frank's RedHot* Sauce, rice and olives. Spoon evenly into bell pepper halves.

Cover; bake 35 minutes or until bell peppers are tender. Uncover; sprinkle with cheese and remaining ⅔ *cup* onions. Bake 1 minute or until onions are golden brown.   *Makes 6 servings*

Prep Time: 10 minutes
Cook Time: 36 minutes

Zesty Italian Stuffed Pepper

Orange-Roasted Turkey Pot Roast and Vegetables

1½ pounds JENNIE-O TURKEY STORE® Turkey Breast Roast
8 medium-size red new potatoes, cut in quarters
1 cup frozen pearl onions or 2 small onions, cut in wedges
2 medium carrots cut in quarters lengthwise, then in 2-inch pieces
   Salt and pepper
1 medium orange
1 cup chicken broth
½ teaspoon *each* minced garlic and crushed dried rosemary
1 package (9 ounces) frozen artichoke hearts, thawed and separated
1 jar (2 ounces) pimiento-stuffed olives, drained
   Fresh rosemary and grated orange peel (optional)

Heat oven to 350°F. In roasting pan, place turkey roast, pop-up timer on top. Surround turkey with potatoes, onions and carrots. Season with salt and pepper to taste. Grate peel from orange, then squeeze juice and pour broth over meat and vegetables. Sprinkle with garlic and rosemary. Bring mixture to a boil on rangetop; cover roasting pan and place in oven. Bake 30 minutes. Stir artichokes and olives into vegetables. Bake until timer pops, 10 to 20 minutes longer. Remove roast and vegetables to serving platter. Place roasting pan over high heat and boil juices until reduced by half. To serve, spoon juices over sliced turkey and vegetables. Garnish with fresh rosemary and grated orange peel, if desired.   *Makes 4 to 5 servings*

Note: If you're doubling the recipe and using a larger roast (3 to 4 pounds), don't add potatoes, onions and carrots until roast has cooked for an hour, or the vegetables will be overcooked. Baste the vegetables with pan drippings after adding them, then continue cooking as directed in recipe.

Cook Time: 1 hour

Easy Chicken and Mushroom Stroganoff

4 boneless, skinless chicken breast halves
2 tablespoons butter
2 tablespoons all-purpose flour
1 medium red onion, chopped
8 ounces mushrooms, quartered
1½ cups chicken broth
2 tablespoons prepared coarse-grain mustard
½ cup sour cream
3 tablespoons chopped fresh parsley
2 cups cooked egg noodles

In large nonstick frypan, melt butter over high heat. Place flour in pie pan; add chicken and turn to coat well. Place chicken in frypan and cook, turning about 5 minutes to brown well on both sides. Stir in onion, mushrooms and any remaining flour. Reduce heat to medium and cook, stirring, until onion is golden brown, about 5 minutes.

In small bowl, whisk together chicken broth and mustard. Pour mixture into frypan and stir. Bring to a boil; reduce heat and simmer about 5 minutes. Stir in sour cream and parsley; simmer for 2 additional minutes. Season with salt and pepper to taste.

Serve over egg noodles.   *Makes 4 servings*

Tip: To freeze, transfer stroganoff to plastic container with tight-fitting lid. Let cool, uncovered, for 20 minutes. Refrigerate, uncovered, until cold, about 30 minutes. Cover tightly and freeze until needed. To thaw, transfer from freezer to refrigerator 12 to 24 hours before needed. Reheat in large, covered frypan over medium-low heat. Bring to a simmer and cook about 5 minutes.

Favorite recipe from **National Chicken Council**

Easy Chicken and Mushroom Stroganoff

Double Cheese Veal Cutlets

2 tablespoons butter
1 pound veal cutlets
  Salt and black pepper
4 cups CLAMATO® Tomato Cocktail
  Pinch of dried thyme
2 tablespoons grated Parmesan cheese
1 cup (4 ounces) shredded Swiss cheese
1 avocado, peeled and sliced

1. In large skillet, melt butter. Brown cutlets a few at a time, 2 minutes on each side. Remove and sprinkle lightly with salt and pepper.

2. Return veal to skillet, overlapping cutlets. Add Clamato and thyme; simmer 5 to 10 minutes, or until veal is tender. Arrange veal in ovenproof serving dish and pour sauce over veal. Sprinkle with Parmesan cheese and Swiss cheese. Place under preheated broiler 5 minutes, or until cheese is melted. Top cutlets with avocado slices. *Makes 6 to 8 servings*

Grilled Apple-Stuffed Pork Chops

5 tablespoons *French's*® Spicy Brown Mustard, divided
3 tablespoons honey, divided
1 cup corn bread stuffing mix
1 small McIntosh apple, peeled, cored and chopped
¼ cup minced onion
¼ cup chopped fresh parsley
4 rib pork chops, cut 1¼ inches thick (about 2 pounds)

1. Combine *¼ cup water*, 2 tablespoons mustard and 1 tablespoon honey in medium bowl. Add stuffing mix, apple, onion and parsley; toss until crumbs are moistened. Combine remaining 3 tablespoons mustard and 2 tablespoons honey in small bowl; set aside for glaze.

2. Cut horizontal slits in pork chops, using sharp knife, to make pockets for stuffing. Spoon stuffing evenly into pockets. Secure openings with toothpicks.

3. Place pork chops on oiled grid. Grill over medium heat 40 to 45 minutes until no longer pink near bone, turning often. Baste chops with reserved glaze during last 10 minutes of cooking. *Makes 4 servings*

Prep Time: 20 minutes
Cook Time: 40 minutes

Double Cheese Veal Cutlets

No-Peek Skillet Chicken

    2 tablespoons BERTOLLI® Olive Oil
    1 chicken (2½ to 3 pounds), cut into serving pieces (with or without skin)
    1 can (14½ ounces) whole peeled tomatoes, undrained and chopped
    ½ cup sliced fresh or drained canned mushrooms
    1 clove garlic, minced
    1 envelope LIPTON® RECIPE SECRETS® Onion Soup Mix*
      Hot cooked noodles

Also terrific with LIPTON® RECIPE SECRETS® Savory Herb with Garlic or Beefy Onion Soup Mix.

In 12-inch skillet, heat oil over medium-high heat and brown chicken; drain. Stir in tomatoes, mushrooms and garlic combined with onion soup mix. Reduce heat to low and simmer covered 25 minutes or until chicken is thoroughly cooked. Serve over hot noodles and sprinkle, if desired, with chopped fresh parsley.   *Makes about 6 servings*

Menu Suggestion: Serve with a mixed green salad and Lipton® Iced Tea.

Cavemen Beef Back Ribs

    ¼ cup paprika
    ¼ cup brown sugar
    ¼ cup seasoned salt
    2 full racks beef back ribs, split in half (about 6 to 8 pounds)
    1 cup *Cattlemen's®* Authentic Smoke House Barbecue Sauce
    ¼ cup apple, pineapple or orange juice

1. Combine paprika, sugar and seasoned salt. Rub mixture into ribs. Cover ribs and refrigerate 1 to 3 hours.

2. Prepare grill for indirect cooking over medium-low heat (250°F). Place ribs on rib rack or in foil pan. Cook on covered grill 2½ to 3 hours until very tender.

3. Meanwhile, combine barbecue sauce and juice. Brush mixture on ribs during last 30 minutes of cooking. Serve with additional barbecue sauce.   *Makes 6 to 8 servings*

Tip: For very tender ribs, remove membrane from underside of ribs before cooking. With a sharp paring knife, score membrane on bone from underside of ribs. Lift up portions of membrane with point of knife. Using kitchen towel, pull membrane away from bone and discard.

Prep Time: 5 minutes
Cook Time: 3 hours
Marinate Time: 1 hour

No-Peek Skillet Chicken

Grilling Greats

Everything tastes better when it's kissed with smoke and cooked out in the open air. The grill can turn weeknight burgers into a gourmet treat or help transform ordinary boneless, skinless chicken breasts into delectable Spicy Mango Chicken. Grilling is one of the easiest and quickest ways to make the most of natural flavors (and you won't even have pots and pans to wash). From simple Beef Kabobs with Apricot Glaze to fun and funky Cajun BBQ Beer Can Chicken, you'll find recipes in this chapter that will light your fire.

Mojo Pork with Orange-Apple Salsa (page 215)

Spicy Margarita Shrimp

⅔ cup *Frank's® Redhot® Chile 'n Lime*™ Hot Sauce
¼ cup olive oil
2 tablespoons lime juice
1 teaspoon grated lime zest
2 teaspoons minced garlic
1½ pounds jumbo shrimp, shelled and deveined
1 (16 ounce) jar mild chunky salsa
2 tablespoons minced cilantro
2 red or orange bell peppers, cut into chunks

1. Whisk together *Chile 'n Lime*™ Hot Sauce, oil, lime juice, zest and garlic. Place shrimp into resealable plastic bag. Pour ⅔ cup marinade over shrimp. Seal bag; marinate in refrigerator 30 minutes.

2. Combine remaining marinade with salsa and cilantro in bowl; set aside.

3. Place shrimp and bell pepper chunks on metal skewers. Grill over medium-high direct heat about 8 minutes until shrimp turn pink. Serve with spicy salsa on the side.

Makes 4 to 6 servings

Tip: To make Mesa Grill BBQ Sauce, add ½ cup *Frank's® Redhot® Chile 'n Lime*™ Hot Sauce to 1 cup *Cattlemen's®* Authentic Smoke House Barbecue Sauce.

Prep Time: 10 minutes
Cook Time: 8 minutes
Marinate Time: 30 minutes

Spicy Margarita Shrimp

Grilled Sherry Pork Chops

¼ cup HOLLAND HOUSE® Sherry Cooking Wine
¼ cup GRANDMA'S® Molasses
2 tablespoons soy sauce
4 pork chops (1 inch thick)

In plastic bowl, combine sherry, molasses and soy sauce; pour over pork chops. Cover; refrigerate 30 minutes. Prepare grill. Drain pork chops; reserve marinade. Grill pork chops over medium-high heat 20 to 30 minutes or until pork is no longer pink in center, turning once and brushing frequently with reserved marinade.* Discard any remaining marinade.   *Makes 4 servings*

Do not baste during last 5 minutes of grilling.

Maple-Mustard-Glazed Spareribs

4 pounds pork spareribs
½ teaspoon salt
½ teaspoon pickling spices*
2 teaspoons vegetable oil
1 small onion, coarsely chopped
½ cup maple-flavored syrup
¼ cup cider vinegar
2 tablespoons water
1 tablespoon Dijon mustard
  Dash salt
¼ teaspoon black pepper

Pickling spices is a blend of seasonings used for pickling foods. It can include allspice, bay leaves, cardamom, coriander, cinnamon, cloves, ginger, mustard seeds and/or pepper. Most supermarkets carry prepackaged pickling spices in the spice aisle.

Sprinkle spareribs with ½ teaspoon salt. Place pickling spices in several thicknesses of cheesecloth; tie up to make a bouquet garni. Set aside. For glaze, heat oil in small saucepan; add onion. Cook and stir until tender. Add bouquet garni. Stir in syrup, vinegar, water, mustard, dash salt and pepper. Bring to a boil over medium-high heat; reduce heat to low and simmer 20 minutes. Discard bouquet garni.

Prepare grill with rectangular foil drip pan. Bank briquets on either side of drip pan for indirect cooking. Place ribs on grid over drip pan. Grill, on covered grill, over low coals 1½ hours or until ribs are tender, turning and basting occasionally with glaze. (Do not baste during last 5 minutes of grilling.)   *Makes 4 servings*

*Favorite recipe from **National Pork Board***

Grilled Sherry Pork Chop

Blue Cheese Burgers with Red Onion

    2 pounds ground beef chuck
    2 cloves garlic, minced
    1 teaspoon salt
    ½ teaspoon black pepper
    4 ounces blue cheese
    ⅓ cup coarsely chopped walnuts, toasted
    1 torpedo (long) red onion *or* 2 small red onions, sliced into ⅜-inch-thick rounds
    2 baguettes (each 12 inches long)
      Olive or vegetable oil

Combine beef, garlic, salt and pepper in medium bowl. Shape meat mixture into 12 oval patties. Mash cheese and blend with walnuts in small bowl. Divide cheese mixture equally; place on centers of 6 meat patties. Top with remaining meat patties; tightly pinch edges together to seal in filling.

Oil hot grid to help prevent sticking. Grill patties and onion, if desired, on covered grill, over medium KINGSFORD® Briquets, 7 to 12 minutes for medium doneness (160°F), turning once. Cut baguettes into 4-inch lengths; split each piece and brush cut side with olive oil. Move cooked burgers to edge of grill to keep warm. Grill bread, oil side down, until lightly toasted. Serve burgers on toasted baguettes.   *Makes 6 servings*

Marinated Flank Steak with Pineapple

    1 can (15¼ ounces) DEL MONTE® Sliced Pineapple In Its Own Juice
    ¼ cup teriyaki sauce
    2 tablespoons honey
    1 pound beef flank steak

1. Drain pineapple, reserving 2 tablespoons juice. Set aside pineapple for later use.

2. Combine reserved juice, teriyaki sauce and honey in shallow 2-quart dish; mix well. Add meat; turn to coat. Cover and refrigerate at least 30 minutes or overnight.

3. Remove meat from marinade, reserving marinade. Grill meat over hot coals (or broil), brushing occasionally with reserved marinade. Cook about 4 minutes on each side for rare; about 5 minutes on each side for medium; or about 6 minutes on each side for well done. During last 4 minutes of cooking, grill pineapple until heated through.

4. Slice meat across grain; serve with pineapple. Garnish, if desired.   *Makes 4 servings*

Note: Do not baste during last 5 minutes of cooking. Marinade that has come into contact with raw meat must be discarded or boiled for several minutes before serving with cooked food.

Blue Cheese Burger with Red Onion

Asian Grilled Steaks with Spicy Herb Sauce

⅔ cup CRISCO® Oil*
3 tablespoons sugar
3 tablespoons cooking sherry
1 tablespoon plus 1½ teaspoons minced garlic
1 tablespoon dark sesame oil
1 teaspoon red pepper flakes
½ teaspoon salt
6 (1-inch-thick) strip steaks
   Salt and black pepper, to taste

Spicy Herb Sauce
   1 cup chopped cilantro, including stems
   ⅓ cup CRISCO® Oil*
   3 tablespoons soy sauce
   1 tablespoon fresh lime juice
1½ teaspoons minced garlic
   ½ teaspoon dark sesame oil
   ½ teaspoon minced jalapeño pepper**

*Use your favorite Crisco Oil.

**Jalapeño peppers can sting and irritate the skin; wear rubber gloves when handling peppers and do not touch your eyes.

Stir together CRISCO Oil, sugar, sherry, garlic, sesame oil, red pepper flakes and salt in a 13×9-inch baking dish. Stir until sugar is dissolved. Season steaks with salt and black pepper. Add steaks, turning once to coat. Marinate for 1 hour in refrigerator, turning once.

To make Spicy Herb Sauce, stir together cilantro, CRISCO Oil, soy sauce, lime juice, garlic, sesame oil and jalapeño; set aside.

Preheat grill.

Remove steaks from marinade. Discard marinade. Cook steaks on a medium-hot grill for 3 to 4 minutes per side for medium-rare or until desired doneness. Top each steak with sauce.

Makes 6 servings

Asian Grilled Steak with Spicy Herb Sauce

Spicy Mango Chicken

¼ **cup mango nectar**
¼ **cup chopped fresh cilantro**
2 **jalapeño chile peppers, seeded and finely chopped**
2 **teaspoons vegetable oil**
2 **teaspoons LAWRY'S® Seasoned Salt**
½ **teaspoon LAWRY'S® Garlic Powder with Parsley**
½ **teaspoon ground cumin**
4 **boneless, skinless chicken breasts (about 1 pound)**
   Mango & Black Bean Salsa (recipe follows)

In small bowl, combine all ingredients except chicken and salsa; mix well. Brush marinade on both sides of chicken. Grill or broil chicken 10 to 15 minutes or until chicken is thoroughly cooked, turning once and basting often with additional marinade. *Do not baste during last 5 minutes of cooking.* Discard any remaining marinade. Top chicken with Mango & Black Bean Salsa.

Makes 4 servings

Hint: Jalapeño peppers can sting and irritate the skin; wear rubber gloves when handling peppers and do not touch eyes.

Mango & Black Bean Salsa

1 **ripe mango, peeled, seeded and chopped**
1 **cup canned black beans, rinsed and drained**
½ **cup chopped tomato**
2 **thinly sliced green onions**
1 **tablespoon chopped fresh cilantro**
1½ **teaspoons lime juice**
1½ **teaspoons red wine vinegar**
½ **teaspoon LAWRY'S® Seasoned Salt**

In medium bowl, combine all ingredients; mix well. Let stand 30 minutes to allow flavors to blend.

Makes about 2¾ cups

Spicy Mango Chicken with Mango & Black Bean Salsa

Tuna Vera Cruz

3 tablespoons tequila, rum or vodka
2 tablespoons lime juice
2 teaspoons grated lime peel
1 piece (1-inch cube) fresh ginger, minced
2 cloves garlic, minced
1 teaspoon salt
1 teaspoon sugar
½ teaspoon ground cumin
¼ teaspoon ground cinnamon
¼ teaspoon black pepper
1 tablespoon vegetable oil
1½ pounds fresh tuna, halibut, swordfish or shark steaks
  Lemon and lime wedges
  Fresh rosemary sprigs

Combine tequila, lime juice, lime peel, ginger, garlic, salt, sugar, cumin, cinnamon and pepper in 2-quart glass dish; stir in oil. Add tuna; turn to coat. Cover and refrigerate at least 30 minutes. Remove tuna from marinade; discard marinade. Grill tuna over medium-hot KINGSFORD® Briquets about 4 minutes per side until fish flakes when tested with fork. Garnish with lemon wedges, lime wedges and rosemary sprigs.   *Makes 4 servings*

Southwest Steak

¾ cup Italian dressing
½ cup minced fresh parsley
⅓ cup *Frank's® RedHot®* Original Cayenne Pepper Sauce
3 tablespoons lime juice
1 tablespoon *French's®* Worcestershire Sauce
2 pounds boneless sirloin or top round steak (1½ inches thick)

1. Place dressing, parsley, **Frank's RedHot** Sauce, lime juice and Worcestershire in blender or food processor. Cover; process until smooth. Reserve ⅔ cup sauce. Pour remaining sauce over steak in deep dish. Cover; refrigerate 30 minutes.

2. Grill or broil steak 8 minutes per side for medium-rare or to desired doneness. Let stand 5 minutes. Slice steak and serve with reserved sauce.   *Makes 6 to 8 servings*

Prep Time: 10 minutes
Marinate Time: 30 minutes
Cook Time: 20 minutes

Tuna Vera Cruz

Blackened Catfish with Creole Vegetables

⅔ cup *Cattlemen's*® Authentic Smoke House Barbecue Sauce or *Cattlemen's* Award Winning Classic Barbecue Sauce
⅓ cup *Frank's*® *Redhot*® *Chile 'n Lime*™ Hot Sauce or *Frank's*® *Redhot*® Cayenne Pepper Sauce
2 tablespoons Southwest chile seasoning blend or Cajun blend seasoning
1 tablespoon olive oil
4 skinless catfish or sea bass fillets (1½ pounds)
   Salt and pepper to taste
   Creole Vegetables (recipe follows)

1. Combine barbecue sauce, *Chile 'n Lime*™ Hot Sauce, seasoning blend and oil. Reserve ½ cup mixture for Creole Vegetables.

2. Season fish with salt and pepper to taste. Baste fish with remaining barbecue mixture.

3. Cook fish on a well greased grill over medium direct heat 5 minutes per side until fish is opaque in center, turning once. Serve with Creole Vegetables.   *Makes 4 servings*

Creole Vegetables

1 red, green or orange bell pepper, cut into quarters
1 large zucchini or summer squash, cut in half crosswise, then lengthwise into thick slices
1 large white onion, sliced ½-inch thick
   Vegetable cooking spray

Arrange vegetables on skewers. Coat vegetables with cooking spray. Grill vegetables over medium direct heat until lightly charred and tender, basting often with reserved ½ cup barbecue sauce mixture.   *Makes 4 servings*

Blackened Catfish with Creole Vegetables

Chicken Thighs with Ginger-Lime Marinade

¾ cup WISH-BONE® Italian Dressing*
2½ tablespoons honey
4 teaspoons lime juice
1 teaspoon ground ginger
¼ teaspoon crushed red pepper flakes (optional)
6 medium chicken thighs (about 2 pounds)

Also terrific with WISH-BONE® Robusto Italian Dressing.

For marinade, combine all ingredients except chicken. In large, shallow, nonaluminum baking dish or plastic bag, pour ¾ cup marinade over chicken; turn to coat. Cover, or close bag, and marinate in refrigerator, turning occasionally, 3 to 24 hours. Refrigerate remaining marinade.

Remove chicken from marinade, discarding marinade. Grill or broil chicken, turning once and brushing frequently with refrigerated marinade, 12 minutes or until chicken is thoroughly cooked.
Makes 4 servings

Drunken T-Bone Steak

2 T-bone steaks, cut 1-inch thick (about 3 pounds)
1 cup *French's®* Worcestershire Sauce
½ cup *Cattlemen's®* Authentic Smoke House Barbecue Sauce
3 tablespoons bourbon
2 tablespoons butter
2 tablespoons *French's®* Worcestershire Sauce
4 teaspoons garlic and pepper steak seasoning

1. Place steaks into resealable plastic food storage bag. Pour 1 cup Worcestershire over steaks. Marinate in refrigerator 1 to 3 hours.

2. Meanwhile, prepare sauce. Combine barbecue sauce, bourbon, butter and 2 tablespoons Worcestershire in saucepan. Heat to boiling. Simmer 3 minutes; reserve.

3. Drain steaks. Rub steak seasoning into meat, coating both sides. Cook steaks over high direct heat, about 7 minutes per side for medium-rare or to desired doneness. Let steaks rest 10 minutes before slicing. Serve with sauce on the side.
Makes 4 servings

Prep Time: 5 minutes
Cook Time: 15 minutes
Marinate Time: 1 hour

Chicken Thighs with Ginger-Lime Marinade

Western Lamb Riblets

   5 pounds lamb riblets, cut into serving-size pieces
¾ cup bottled chili sauce
½ cup beer
½ cup honey
¼ cup Worcestershire sauce
¼ cup finely chopped onion
   1 clove garlic, minced
½ teaspoon crushed red pepper flakes

Trim excess fat from riblets. In saucepan, combine chili sauce, beer, honey, Worcestershire sauce, onion, garlic and pepper flakes. Bring mixture to a boil. Reduce heat; simmer, covered, 10 minutes. Remove from heat; cool.

Place riblets in resealable plastic food storage bag. Pour cooled marinade over riblets in bag. Close bag securely and refrigerate about 2 hours, turning bag occasionally to distribute marinade evenly.

Drain riblets; reserve marinade. Arrange medium-hot KINGSFORD® Briquets around drip pan. Place riblets on grid over drip pan. Cover grill; cook 45 minutes, turning riblets and brushing with marinade twice. Bring remaining marinade to a boil; boil 1 minute. Serve with riblets.

Makes 6 servings

Beef Kabobs with Apricot Glaze

   1 can (15¼ ounces) DEL MONTE® Apricot Halves
   1 tablespoon cornstarch
   1 teaspoon Dijon mustard
½ teaspoon dried basil leaves
   1 pound boneless beef top sirloin steak, cut into 1½-inch cubes
   1 small green bell pepper, cut into ¾-inch pieces
   4 medium mushrooms, cut in half
   4 to 8 skewers*

*To prevent burning of wooden skewers, soak skewers in water for 10 minutes before assembling kabobs.

1. Drain apricot syrup into small saucepan. Blend in cornstarch until dissolved. Cook over medium heat, stirring constantly, until thickened. Stir in mustard and basil. Set aside.

2. Thread beef, apricots, green pepper and mushrooms alternately onto skewers; brush with apricot syrup mixture. Grill kabobs over hot coals (or broil) about 5 minutes on each side or to desired doneness, brushing occasionally with additional syrup mixture. Garnish, if desired.

Makes 4 servings

Western Lamb Riblets

Five-Spice Australian Lamb Shoulder Chops and Ruby Grapefruit-Fennel Salad

Chops & Marinade

8 Australian Lamb shoulder chops, trimmed
2 tablespoons red wine
1 tablespoon honey, softened
1 tablespoon soy sauce
1 teaspoon Chinese 5-spice powder*

Salad

1 ruby grapefruit, segmented and pith removed
1 small bulb fennel, white part only, finely sliced
1 bunch watercress
½ bunch cilantro, chopped
1 tablespoon olive oil
1 tablespoon lemon juice
Sea salt and freshly ground pepper, to taste

Serve

Loaf of sourdough bread (optional)

*Chinese 5-spice powder is available in the spice section of most supermarkets. It is usually a blend of anise, cinnamon, star anise, cloves and ginger.

1. Place the lamb chops in a flat dish. Combine the red wine, honey, soy sauce and 5-spice powder and mix well. Pour over the chops, turning chops so they are fully coated in mixture. Cover and marinate 20 minutes or overnight.

2. To make the salad, combine the grapefruit, fennel, watercress and cilantro in a bowl. Whisk together the oil and juice, season with salt and pepper to taste, and toss with the salad.

3. Heat grill to medium and grill the chops, turning occasionally, for 8 to 10 minutes or until cooked as desired.

4. Serve with the salad and a loaf of sourdough bread.   *Makes 4 servings*

Marinate Time: 20 minutes or overnight
Prep Time: 20 minutes
Cook Time: 10 minutes

*Favorite recipe from **Meat and Livestock Australia***

Grilled Lemon Chicken Dijon

⅓ cup **HOLLAND HOUSE® White with Lemon Cooking Wine**
⅓ **cup olive oil**
2 **tablespoons Dijon mustard**
1 **teaspoon dried thyme leaves**
2 **whole chicken breasts, skinned, boned and halved**

In shallow baking dish combine cooking wine, oil, mustard and thyme. Add chicken and turn to coat. Cover; marinate in refrigerator for 1 to 2 hours.

Prepare grill for direct cooking. Drain chicken, reserving marinade. Grill chicken over medium coals 12 to 16 minutes or until cooked through, turning once and basting with marinade.*

Makes 4 servings

*Do not baste during last 5 minutes of grilling.

Grilled Red Snapper with Tangy Citrus Sauce

¾ cup *French's® Gourmayo™* **Creamy Dijon Flavored Light Mayonnaise, divided**
2 **tablespoons orange juice**
2 **tablespoons lime juice**
1 **tablespoon *each* grated orange and lime zest**
1 **tablespoon minced fresh tarragon**
4 **red snapper fillets, about ½-inch thick (1½ pounds)**
  Salt, pepper and paprika to taste

1. Combine ½ cup mayonnaise, orange and lime juices, zests and tarragon in small bowl; set aside.

2. Season fish with salt, pepper and paprika to taste. Baste with remaining ¼ cup mayonnaise.

3. Cook on a well greased grill over medium direct heat 5 minutes per side until fish is opaque in center, turning once. Serve with sauce.

Makes 4 servings

Note: You may substitute salmon, tilapia or seabass fillets. This sauce pairs well with grilled asparagus.

Tip: Two cake racks can be used for grilling fish. Generously coat racks with vegetable cooking spray. Place fish on bottom rack. Cover with second rack. Use long-handled tongs for turning.

Prep Time: 10 minutes
Cook Time: 10 minutes

Grilled Lemon Chicken Dijon

Cajun BBQ Beer-Can Chicken

4 (12 ounce) cans beer or non-alcoholic malt beverage
1½ cups *Cattlemen's*® Award Winning Classic Barbecue Sauce
¾ cup Cajun spice or Southwest seasoning blend, divided
3 whole chickens (3 to 4 pounds each)
12 sprigs fresh thyme

Cajun BBQ Sauce
1 cup *Cattlemen's*® Award Winning Classic Barbecue Sauce
½ cup beer or non-alcoholic malt beverage
¼ cup butter

1. Combine 1 can beer, 1½ cups barbecue sauce and ½ cup spice blend. Following manufacturer's instructions, fill marinade injection needle with marinade. Inject chickens in several places at least 1-inch deep. Place chickens into resealable plastic food storage bags. Pour any remaining marinade over chickens. Seal bag; marinate in refrigerator 1 to 3 hours or overnight.

2. Meanwhile prepare Cajun BBQ Sauce: In saucepan, combine 1 cup barbecue sauce, ½ cup beer, butter and 1 tablespoon spice blend. Simmer 5 minutes. Refrigerate and warm just before serving.

3. Open remaining cans of beer. Spill out about ½ cup beer from each can. Using can opener, punch several holes in tops of cans. Spoon about 1 tablespoon additional spice blend and 4 sprigs thyme into each can. Place 1 can upright into each cavity of chicken, arranging legs forward so chicken stands upright.

4. Place chickens upright over indirect heat on barbecue grill. Cook on a covered grill on medium-high (350°F), about 1½ hours until thigh meat registers 180°F internal temperature. (Cover chickens with foil if they become too brown while cooking.) Let stand 10 minutes before serving. Using tongs, carefully remove cans from chicken. Cut into quarters to serve. Serve with Cajun BBQ Sauce.

Makes 12 servings

Prep Time: 20 minutes
Cook Time: 1½ hours
Marinate Time: 1 hour or overnight

Mojo Pork with Orange-Apple Salsa

    2 tablespoons olive oil
    1 tablespoon minced garlic
    ½ cup *Frank's® Redhot® Chile 'n Lime™* Hot Sauce
    ½ cup orange juice
    2 tablespoons grated orange zest
    ¼ cup minced cilantro
    2 tablespoons chili powder
    1 teaspoon oregano leaves
    2 boneless pork tenderloins (2 pounds)
    ½ cup sour cream
       Orange-Apple Salsa (recipe follows)

1. Sauté garlic in hot oil; cool. Slowly stir in *Chile 'n Lime™* Hot Sauce, orange juice, zest, cilantro, chili powder and oregano. Reserve ¼ cup marinade.

2. Place pork into resealable plastic food storage bags. Pour remaining marinade over pork. Seal bag; marinate in refrigerator 1 to 3 hours. Combine remaining marinade with sour cream; set aside in refrigerator.

3. Grill pork over medium-high direct heat for 30 minutes until no longer pink in center. Slice pork and drizzle with spicy sour cream. Serve with Orange-Apple Salsa.

Makes 6 to 8 servings

Prep Time: 15 minutes
Cook Time: 35 minutes
Marinate Time: 1 hour

Orange-Apple Salsa

    3 navel oranges, peeled, sectioned and cut into small pieces
    2 large apples, cored and cut into small dice
    2 tablespoons chopped red onion
    2 tablespoons chopped cilantro
    2 tablespoons *Frank's® Redhot® Chile 'n Lime™* Hot Sauce

Combine ingredients in bowl; chill until ready to serve.

Makes about 3 cups

Texas Smoked BBQ Brisket

½ cup prepared barbecue seasoning
2 tablespoons ground chili powder
1 (5- to 7-pound) beef brisket, trimmed with a layer of fat (center flat portion)
1 cup *Frank's® Redhot® Chile 'n Lime™* Hot Sauce or *Frank's® Redhot®* Cayenne Pepper
    Sauce
1½ cups beer or non-alcoholic malt beverage, divided
1 cup *Cattlemen's®* Authentic Smoke House Barbecue Sauce or *Cattlemen's®* Award Winning
    Classic Barbecue Sauce
¼ cup butter

1. Combine barbecue seasoning and chili powder. Rub mixture thoroughly into beef. Place meat, fat-side up, in disposable foil pan. Cover and refrigerate 1 to 3 hours. Just before using, prepare mop sauce by combining *Chile 'n Lime™* Hot Sauce and 1 cup beer; set aside.

2. Prepare grill for indirect cooking over medium-low heat (250°F). If desired, toss soaked wood chips over coals or heat source. Place pan with meat in center of grill over indirect heat. Cover grill. Cook meat, over low heat 6 to 7 hours until meat is very tender (190°F internal temperature). Baste with mop sauce once an hour.

3. Combine barbecue sauce, butter and remaining ½ cup beer. Simmer 5 minutes until slightly thickened. Slice meat and serve with sauce.   *Makes 10 to 12 servings*

Tip: To easily slice meat, cut against the grain using an electric knife.

Prep Time: 15 minutes
Cook Time: 7 hours
Marinate Time: 1 hour

Sizzlin' Burgers

1 pound ground beef
¼ cup *French's®* Worcestershire Sauce
½ teaspoon garlic salt

1. Combine ground beef, Worcestershire and garlic salt; shape into 4 burgers.

2. Grill over medium heat for 15 minutes or until no longer pink in center, turning once.

3. Serve burgers on rolls. Splash on more Worcestershire to taste.

Makes 4 servings

Prep Time: 5 minutes
Cook Time: 15 minutes

Texas Smoked BBQ Brisket

Grilled Tequila Lime Shrimp

    1 cup LAWRY'S® Tequila Lime Marinade With Lime Juice, divided
    1 pound large uncooked shrimp, peeled and deveined
    8 wooden skewers, soaked in water for 15 minutes
    1 yellow bell pepper, cut into 1½-inch pieces
    6 green onions, sliced into 1½-inch pieces
   16 cherry or pear tomatoes
    1 lime, sliced into 8 wedges

In large resealable plastic bag, combine ½ cup Lawry's Tequila Lime Marinade with Lime Juice and shrimp; turn to coat. Close bag and marinate in refrigerator 30 minutes. Remove shrimp from Marinade, discarding Marinade.

On wooden skewers, alternately thread shrimp, yellow pepper, onion and tomatoes. Grill brushing frequently with remaining ½ cup Marinade and turning once, until shrimp turn pink. Serve, if desired, with lime wedges and over hot cooked pasta, rice or orzo.

Makes 8 skewers (4 servings)

Variations: Also great served in pita bread or flour tortilla with shredded lettuce and lime juice squeezed over the top. Both ideas are great for picnics and parties!

Prep Time: 15 minutes
Marinate time: 30 minutes
Cook Time: 10 minutes

Herb Garlic Grilled Chicken

    ¼ cup chopped parsley
   1½ tablespoons minced garlic
    4 teaspoons grated lemon peel
    1 tablespoon chopped fresh mint
    1 chicken (2½ to 3 pounds), quartered

Combine parsley, garlic, lemon peel and mint. Loosen skin from breast and thigh portions of chicken quarters by running fingers between skin and meat. Rub some of seasoning mixture evenly over meat under skin, replace skin and rub remaining seasonings over outside of chicken to cover evenly. Arrange medium-hot KINGSFORD® Briquets on one side of covered grill. Place chicken on grid opposite coals. Cover grill and cook chicken 45 to 55 minutes, turning once or twice. Chicken is done when juices run clear.

Makes 4 servings

Grilled Tequila Lime Shrimp

Ethnic Specialties

American cooking has always been a melting pot of flavors—Friday-night Chinese, spaghetti dinners at church, Super Bowl guacamole. These recipes offer a quick world tour of favorite dishes and introduce some delightful new tastes. Sup on classic Spaghetti Bolognese or the Original Ortega® Taco Recipe. If you're feeling more adventurous, try Javanese Pork Saté or Grecian Lamb Kabobs. With all these wonders to tempt your taste buds, you may never serve meat loaf again!

Caribbean Glazed Swordfish
with Grilled Pineapple Chutney
(page 232)

221

Baja Fish Tacos

½ **cup sour cream**
½ **cup mayonnaise**
¼ **cup chopped fresh cilantro**
1 **package (1.25 ounces) ORTEGA® Taco Seasoning Mix,** *divided*
1 **pound (about 4) cod or other white fish fillets, cut into 1-inch pieces**
2 **tablespoons vegetable oil**
2 **tablespoons lemon juice**
1 **package (12) ORTEGA Taco Shells**

Toppings
Shredded cabbage, chopped tomato, lime juice, ORTEGA Taco Sauce

COMBINE sour cream, mayonnaise, cilantro and *2 tablespoons* taco seasoning mix in small bowl.

COMBINE cod, vegetable oil, lemon juice and *remaining* taco seasoning mix in medium bowl; pour into large skillet. Cook, stirring constantly, over medium-high heat for 4 to 5 minutes or until fish flakes easily when tested with fork.

FILL taco shells with fish mixture. Layer with desired toppings. Top with sour cream sauce.

Makes 6 servings

Javanese Pork Saté

1 **pound boneless pork loin**
½ **cup minced onion**
2 **tablespoons peanut butter**
2 **tablespoons lemon juice**
2 **tablespoons soy sauce**
1 **tablespoon brown sugar**
1 **tablespoon vegetable oil**
1 **clove garlic, minced**
Dash hot pepper sauce

Cut pork into ½-inch cubes; place in shallow dish. In blender or food processor combine remaining ingredients. Blend until smooth. Pour over pork. Cover and marinate in refrigerator 10 minutes. Thread pork onto skewers. (If using bamboo skewers, soak in water 1 hour to prevent burning.)

Grill or broil 10 to 12 minutes, turning occasionally, until done. Serve with hot cooked rice, if desired.

Makes 4 servings

Favorite recipe from **National Pork Board**

Baja Fish Tacos

Asian Honey-Tea Grilled Prawns

1½ **pounds medium raw shrimp, peeled and deveined**
    Salt
2 **green onions, thinly sliced**

Marinade
   1 **cup brewed double-strength orange-spice tea, cooled**
  ¼ **cup honey**
  ¼ **cup rice vinegar**
  ¼ **cup soy sauce**
  1 **tablespoon finely chopped fresh ginger**
  ½ **teaspoon ground black pepper**

In plastic bag, combine marinade ingredients. Remove ½ cup marinade; set aside for dipping sauce. Add shrimp to marinade in bag, turning to coat. Close bag securely and marinate in refrigerator 30 minutes or up to 12 hours.

Remove shrimp from marinade; discard marinade. Thread shrimp onto 8 skewers, dividing evenly. Grill over medium coals 4 to 6 minutes or until shrimp turn pink and are just firm to the touch, turning once. Season with salt, as desired.

Meanwhile prepare dipping sauce by placing reserved ½ cup marinade in small saucepan. Bring to a boil over medium-high heat. Boil 3 to 5 minutes or until slightly reduced. Stir in green onions.
Makes 4 servings

Favorite recipe from **National Honey Board**

Cuban Sandwiches

6 **tablespoons** *French's® Classic Yellow®* **Mustard or** *French's®* **Sweet 'n Zesty Mustard**
4 **Portuguese or Kaiser rolls, split in half**
8 **ounces thinly sliced ham**
8 **ounces thinly sliced deli roast pork**
8 **ounces sandwich-style dill pickles**
4 **ounces thinly sliced Swiss or Muenster cheese**

1. Spread mustard on cut sides of rolls. Layer ham, pork, pickles and cheese on bottoms of rolls. Cover with top halves of rolls. With bottom of a heavy skillet, press sandwiches firmly down on work surface to compress bread and filling.

2. Preheat an electric grill pan for 5 minutes. Place sandwiches on pan and close cover. Cook 6 minutes, turning halfway during cooking. Cut in half and serve hot.
Makes 4 servings

Asian Honey-Tea Grilled Prawns

Corned Beef and Cabbage with Parsley Dumplings

1 (4-pound) corned beef brisket, rinsed and trimmed
2 tablespoons TABASCO® brand Green Pepper Sauce
1 small green cabbage, coarsely shredded

Parsley Dumplings
2 cups flour
1 tablespoon baking powder
¼ teaspoon salt
1 cup milk
1 egg, beaten
2 tablespoons chopped fresh parsley
1 tablespoon butter or margarine, melted
2 teaspoons TABASCO® brand Green Pepper Sauce

Place corned beef in large saucepan with enough cold water to cover by 2 inches; add TABASCO® Green Pepper Sauce. Heat to boiling over high heat. Reduce heat to low; cover and simmer 2 hours, occasionally skimming surface.

During last 10 minutes of cooking corned beef, add cabbage to cooking liquid; return to boil over high heat. Reduce heat, cover and simmer 10 minutes or until cabbage is tender. Remove corned beef and cabbage to warm serving platter; keep warm. Reserve liquid in saucepan.

For Parsley Dumplings, combine flour, baking powder and salt in large bowl. Whisk milk, egg, parsley, butter and TABASCO® Green Pepper Sauce in small bowl until blended. Stir milk mixture into dry ingredients just until blended. Form dumplings by dropping tablespoonfuls of batter into reserved simmering liquid. Cover and simmer 10 minutes or until dumplings are cooked in center. Transfer dumplings to platter with corned beef and cabbage using slotted spoon.

Makes 6 to 8 servings

Corned Beef and Cabbage with Parsley Dumplings

Spaghetti Bolognese

½ pound lean ground beef plus ½ pound bulk Italian sausage (or all ground beef)
3 tablespoons CRISCO® Oil
½ pound mushrooms, sliced
1 large onion, diced
1 tablespoon jarred minced garlic (or 2 large cloves garlic, peeled and minced)
1 teaspoon salt
1 teaspoon freshly ground black pepper
1 can (14½ ounces) diced tomatoes
1 can (15 ounces) tomato sauce
1 teaspoon dried basil
1 teaspoon dried oregano
½ teaspoon crushed red pepper flakes
¾ pound uncooked spaghetti
   Freshly grated Parmesan cheese (optional)

Use your favorite Crisco Oil.

1. Heat large skillet on medium-high heat. Add beef and sausage. Break up chunks with fork. Cook until no longer pink. Remove from pan with slotted spoon. Set aside. Discard drippings from pan.

2. Return skillet to medium-high heat. Heat CRISCO Oil. Add mushrooms, onion and garlic. Sauté until onion is translucent. Stir in salt and pepper.

3. Return beef to pan. Add tomatoes, tomato sauce, basil, oregano and crushed red pepper flakes. Bring to a boil. Reduce heat to low. Simmer sauce 20 to 30 minutes; stirring occasionally.

4. While sauce simmers, cook pasta according to package directions. Drain. Top with sauce. Serve with cheese, if desired.

Makes 4 servings

Thai Curry Coconut Pork Chops

　1 tablespoon vegetable oil
¼ cup *each* minced green onion and yellow onion
½ cup *Cattlemen's®* Golden Honey Barbecue Sauce
½ cup cream of coconut (not coconut milk)
¼ cup *Frank's® Redhot® Chile 'n Lime™* Hot Sauce
　2 teaspoons grated peeled ginger root
½ teaspoon curry powder
¼ cup heavy cream
　6 rib cut bone-in pork chops, cut 1-inch thick, seasoned with salt and pepper to taste

1. Prepare Thai Curry Coconut Sauce: Heat oil in small saucepan; sauté onions just until tender. Add barbecue sauce, cream of coconut, *Chile 'n Lime™* Hot Sauce, ginger and curry powder. Simmer 5 minutes until slightly thickened. Transfer ¾ cup sauce to bowl for basting. Add cream to remaining sauce. Simmer 3 minutes; keep warm.

2. Grill chops over medium direct heat 25 minutes or until no longer pink near bone, basting with chile sauce mixture during last 10 minutes of cooking.

3. Arrange chops on serving platter. Serve with Thai Curry Coconut Sauce and, if desired, steamed jasmine rice.

Makes 6 servings

Tip: For a colorful presentation, toss cooked rice with minced red onion and parsley.

Prep Time: 5 minutes
Cook Time: 30 minutes

Thai Curry Coconut Pork Chop

Ortega® Green Chile Guacamole

2 medium very ripe avocados, seeded, peeled and mashed
1 can (4 ounces) ORTEGA® Diced Green Chiles
2 large green onions, chopped
2 tablespoons olive oil
1 teaspoon lime juice
1 clove garlic, finely chopped
¼ teaspoon salt
   Tortilla chips

COMBINE avocados, chiles, green onions, olive oil, lime juice, garlic and salt in medium bowl. Cover; refrigerate for at least 1 hour. Serve with chips. *Makes 2 cups*

Caribbean Glazed Swordfish with Grilled Pineapple Chutney

½ cup *Frank's® Redhot®* Cayenne Pepper Sauce or *Frank's® Redhot®* XTRA Hot Cayenne Pepper Sauce
¼ cup packed light brown sugar
1 teaspoon dried thyme leaves
½ teaspoon ground allspice
2 tablespoons olive oil
4 swordfish steaks, 1-inch thick, seasoned with salt and pepper to taste
   Grilled Pineapple Chutney (recipe follows)

Whisk together *Frank's® Redhot®* Sauce, sugar, thyme and allspice. Reserve 3 tablespoons mixture for Grilled Pineapple Chutney. Mix oil into remaining spice mixture; thoroughly baste fish. Place fish on well-greased grill. Cook, covered, over medium-high direct heat for 10 to 15 minutes until opaque in center, turning once. Serve with Grilled Pineapple Chutney. *Makes 4 servings*

Grilled Pineapple Chutney

½ of a fresh pineapple, peeled and sliced ½-inch thick
1 red or orange bell pepper, cut into quarters
2 tablespoons minced red onion
1 tablespoon *each* minced candied ginger and minced cilantro

Grill pineapple and bell pepper 10 minutes over medium-high direct heat until tender. Chop; place in bowl with reserved hot sauce mixture, onion, ginger and cilantro. *Makes 3 cups*

Ortega® Green Chile Guacamole

Grecian Lamb Kabobs

　　1 cup dry white wine
　¼ cup olive oil
　24 bay leaves
　12 pieces lemon peel, about 3 inches, cut in half
　　2 medium onions, peeled, cut into 9 wedges and wedges cut in half
　½ teaspoon salt
　¼ teaspoon black pepper
　　2 pounds boneless leg of American lamb, cut into 1-inch cubes
　12 cherry tomatoes
　　2 green peppers, cut into 12 pieces, cut pieces in half
　　　Minted orzo (recipe follows)

Combine wine, olive oil, bay leaves, lemon peel, onions, salt and black pepper in large bowl. Pour into large resealable plastic food storage bag. Add lamb to marinade. Marinate overnight; turn lamb once.

Alternate lamb, bay leaves and lemon peel on skewers. On separate skewers, alternate peppers and onions; brush kabobs with marinade.

Boil remaining marinade 1 minute. Broil lamb kabobs and vegetable kabobs 5 to 7 minutes each side. Add tomato to end of each lamb kabob during last 3 minutes of cooking. Baste with marinade throughout cooking. Serve with Minted Orzo.　　　　　*Makes 6 servings*

*Favorite recipe from **American Lamb Council***

Minted Orzo

　　1 package (12 ounces) orzo*
　　2 tablespoons chopped fresh mint
　　2 teaspoons grated lemon peel
　　　Salt and pepper to taste

*Orzo is a Greek, rice-shaped pasta found in the pasta or specialty aisles in most supermarkets.

Cook orzo in boiling water about 5 minutes. Drain and toss with remaining ingredients.

*Favorite recipe from **American Lamb Council***

Grecian Lamb Kabobs

Fish Françoise

 1 can (14½ ounces) DEL MONTE® Diced Tomatoes with Garlic & Onion
 1 tablespoon lemon juice
 2 cloves garlic, minced
 ½ teaspoon dried tarragon leaves
 ⅛ teaspoon black pepper
 3 tablespoons whipping cream
   Vegetable oil
 1½ pounds firm white fish fillets (such as halibut or cod)
   Salt
   Lemon wedges

1. Preheat broiler; position rack 4 inches from heat.

2. Combine undrained tomatoes, lemon juice, garlic, tarragon and pepper in large saucepan. Cook over medium-high heat about 10 minutes or until liquid has evaporated.

3. Stir in cream. Reduce heat to low. Cook until tomato mixture is very thick; set aside.

4. Brush broiler pan with oil. Arrange fish on pan; season with salt and additional pepper, if desired. Broil 3 to 4 minutes on each side or until fish flakes easily when tested with a fork.

5. Spread tomato mixture over top of fish. Broil 1 minute. Serve with lemon wedges.

Makes 4 servings

Skillet Shrimp Scampi

 2 teaspoons BERTOLLI® Olive Oil
 2 pounds uncooked shrimp, peeled and deveined
 ⅔ cup LAWRY'S® Herb & Garlic Marinade
 ¼ cup finely chopped green onion, including tops

In large nonstick skillet, heat oil over medium heat. Add shrimp and Herb & Garlic Marinade. Cook, stirring often, until shrimp turn pink, about 3 to 5 minutes. Stir in green onions.

Makes 4 to 6 servings

Meal Idea: Serve over hot, cooked rice, orzo or your favorite pasta.

Variations: This dish is wonderful served chilled with toothpicks as an appetizer. Try serving chilled then tossed in a pasta or green salad. Take it to your next picnic! Also delicious using LAWRY'S® Lemon Pepper Marinade.

Fish Françoise

Stuffed Pork Loin Genoa Style

1 (4- to 5-pound) boneless pork loin roast
1¼ cups fresh parsley, chopped and divided
½ cup fresh basil leaves, chopped
½ cup pine nuts
½ cup grated Parmesan cheese
6 cloves garlic, peeled and chopped
½ pound ground pork
½ pound Italian sausage
1 cup dry bread crumbs
¼ cup milk
1 egg
1 teaspoon ground black pepper

In food processor or blender, process 1 cup parsley, basil, pine nuts, Parmesan cheese and garlic. Set aside.

Mix together ground pork, Italian sausage, bread crumbs, milk, egg, remaining ¼ cup parsley and pepper.

Place roast fat-side down on cutting board. Spread with the herb-cheese mixture; place ground pork mixture along center of loin. Fold in half; tie with kitchen string. Roast on rack in shallow baking pan at 350°F for 1½ hours or until internal temperature reaches 155°F. Slice to serve.

Makes 10 servings

Prep Time: 15 minutes
Cook Time: 90 minutes

*Favorite recipe from **National Pork Board***

Stuffed Pork Loin Genoa Style

Kung Pao Chicken

   1 pound boneless, skinless chicken breasts, cut into 1-inch pieces
   1 tablespoon cornstarch
   2 teaspoons CRISCO® Oil*
   3 tablespoons chopped green onions with tops
   2 cloves garlic, minced
   ¼ to 1½ teaspoons crushed red pepper
   ¼ to ½ teaspoon ground ginger
   ¼ cup rice vinegar
   ¼ cup soy sauce
   1 tablespoon sugar
   ⅓ cup unsalted dry roasted peanuts
   4 cups hot cooked rice (cooked without salt or fat)

*Use your favorite Crisco Oil.

1. Combine chicken and cornstarch in small bowl; toss. Heat oil in large skillet or wok on medium-high heat. Add chicken. Stir-fry 5 to 7 minutes or until no longer pink in center. Remove from skillet. Add onions, garlic, red pepper and ginger to skillet. Stir-fry 15 seconds. Remove from heat.

2. Combine vinegar, soy sauce and sugar in small bowl. Stir well. Add to skillet. Return chicken to skillet. Stir until coated. Stir in nuts. Heat thoroughly, stirring occasionally. Serve over hot rice.

Makes 4 servings

Carne Asada

   1½ pounds top sirloin steak
   ¼ cup lemon juice
   2 tablespoons vegetable oil
   1 tablespoon chopped fresh cilantro (optional)
   2 teaspoons LAWRY'S® Garlic Salt
   1 teaspoon LAWRY'S® Seasoned Pepper
   1 teaspoon LAWRY'S® Seasoned Salt

Place steak in large resealable plastic bag. Add remaining ingredients and shake to mix; marinate in refrigerator for 30 minutes to overnight. Remove steak from bag, discarding used marinade mixture. Grill or broil steak until cooked to desired doneness, about 5 minutes on each side. Shake on additional Garlic Salt during cooking for extra flavor. *Makes 4 servings*

Prep Time: 5 minutes
Marinate Time: 30 minutes
Cook Time: 10 minutes

Kung Pao Chicken

German-Style Bratwurst & Sauerkraut

6 slices bacon
1 small onion, chopped
1 clove garlic, minced
1 (32-ounce) jar or can sauerkraut, rinsed and well drained
2 medium potatoes, peeled and sliced
1½ to 2 cups water
½ cup apple juice or dry white wine
2 tablespoons brown sugar
1 teaspoon instant chicken bouillon granules
1 teaspoon caraway seeds
1 dried bay leaf
1 pound BOB EVANS® Bratwurst (5 links)
2 medium apples, cored and sliced
Fresh bay leaves (optional)

Cook bacon in large skillet over medium-high heat until crisp. Remove bacon; drain and crumble on paper towel. Set aside. Drain off all but 2 tablespoons drippings in skillet. Add onion and garlic to drippings; cook over medium heat until tender, stirring occasionally. Stir in sauerkraut, potatoes, 1½ cups water, apple juice, brown sugar, bouillon, caraway and dried bay leaf. Add remaining ½ cup water, if necessary, to cover potatoes. Bring to a boil over high heat.

Meanwhile, make 3 or 4 diagonal ¼-inch-deep cuts into one side of each bratwurst. Cook bratwurst in large skillet over medium heat until browned, turning occasionally. Add bratwurst to sauerkraut mixture. Reduce heat to low; simmer, covered, 20 to 30 minutes or until potatoes are just tender, stirring occasionally. Add apples; cook, covered, 5 to 10 minutes or until apples are just tender. Stir in reserved bacon. Remove and discard dried bay leaf. Garnish with fresh bay leaves, if desired. Serve hot. Refrigerate leftovers. *Makes 5 servings*

German-Style Bratwurst & Sauerkraut

Sweet and Sour Pork

¾ **pound boneless pork**
1 **teaspoon vegetable oil**
1 **bag (16 ounces) BIRDS EYE® frozen Pepper Stir Fry vegetables**
1 **tablespoon water**
1 **jar (14 ounces) sweet and sour sauce**
1 **can (8 ounces) pineapple chunks, drained**

• Cut pork into thin strips.

• In large skillet, heat oil over medium-high heat.

• Add pork; stir-fry until pork is browned.

• Add vegetables and water; cover and cook over medium heat 5 to 7 minutes or until vegetables are crisp-tender.

• Uncover; stir in sweet and sour sauce and pineapple. Cook until heated through.

Makes 4 servings

Serving Suggestion: Serve over hot cooked rice.

Birds Eye Idea: For a quick sweet and sour sauce for chicken nuggets or egg rolls, add sugar and vinegar to taste to jarred strained apricots or peaches.

Prep Time: 5 minutes
Cook Time: 15 to 18 minutes

Original Ortega® Taco Recipe

1 **pound ground beef**
1 **package (1¼ ounces) ORTEGA® Taco Seasoning Mix**
¾ **cup water**
1 **package (12) ORTEGA Taco Shells, warmed**

Suggested Toppings
   Shredded lettuce, chopped tomatoes, shredded cheddar cheese, ORTEGA Thick & Smooth Taco Sauce

BROWN beef; drain. Stir in seasoning mix and water; bring to a boil. Reduce heat to low; cook, stirring occasionally, for 5 to 6 minutes or until mixture is thickened.

FILL taco shells with beef mixture. Top with desired toppings.

Makes 6 servings

Sweet and Sour Pork

Chicken Tikka (Tandoori-Style Grilled Chicken)

2 chickens (3 pounds each), cut up
1 pint nonfat yogurt
½ cup *Frank's®* *RedHot®* Original Cayenne Pepper Sauce
1 tablespoon grated peeled fresh ginger
3 cloves garlic, minced
1 tablespoon paprika
1 tablespoon cumin seeds, crushed *or* 1½ teaspoons ground cumin
2 teaspoons salt
1 teaspoon ground coriander

1. Remove skin and visible fat from chicken pieces. Rinse with cold water and pat dry. Randomly poke chicken all over with tip of sharp knife. Place chicken in resealable plastic food storage bags or large glass bowl. Combine yogurt, *Frank's RedHot* Sauce, ginger, garlic, paprika, cumin, salt and coriander in small bowl; mix well. Pour over chicken pieces, turning pieces to coat evenly. Seal bags or cover bowl and marinate in refrigerator 1 hour or overnight.

2. Place chicken on oiled grid, reserving marinade. Grill over medium coals 45 minutes or until chicken is no longer pink near bone and juices run clear, turning and basting often with marinade. (Do not baste during last 10 minutes of cooking.) Discard any remaining marinade. Serve warm.   *Makes 6 servings*

Prep Time: 15 minutes
Marinate Time: 1 hour
Cook Time: 45 minutes

Chicken Tikka (Tandoori-Style Grilled Chicken)

Paella

¼ cup FILIPPO BERIO® Olive Oil
1 pound boneless skinless chicken breasts, cut into 1-inch strips
½ pound Italian sausage, cut into 1-inch slices
1 onion, chopped
3 cloves garlic, minced
2 (14½-ounce) cans chicken broth
2 cups uncooked long grain white rice
1 (8-ounce) bottle clam juice
1 (2-ounce) jar chopped pimientos, drained
2 bay leaves
1 teaspoon salt
¼ teaspoon saffron threads, crumbled (optional)
1 pound raw shrimp, shelled and deveined
1 (16-ounce) can whole tomatoes, drained
1 (10-ounce) package frozen peas, thawed
12 littleneck clams, scrubbed
¼ cup water
Fresh herb sprig (optional)

Preheat oven to 350°F. In large skillet, heat olive oil over medium heat until hot. Add chicken; cook and stir 8 to 10 minutes or until brown on all sides. Remove with slotted spoon; set aside. Add sausage to skillet; cook and stir 8 to 10 minutes or until brown. Remove with slotted spoon; set aside. Add onion and garlic to skillet; cook and stir 5 to 7 minutes or until onion is tender. Transfer chicken, sausage, onion and garlic mixture to large casserole.

Add chicken broth, rice, clam juice, pimientos, bay leaves, salt and saffron, if desired, to chicken mixture. Cover; bake 30 minutes. Add shrimp, tomatoes and peas; stir well. Cover; bake an additional 15 minutes or until rice is tender, liquid is absorbed and shrimp are opaque. Remove bay leaves.

Meanwhile, combine clams and water in stockpot or large saucepan. Cover; cook over medium heat 5 to 10 minutes or until clams open; remove clams immediately as they open. Discard any clams with unopened shells. Place clams on top of paella. Garnish with herb sprig, if desired.

Makes 4 to 6 servings

Paella

Marvelous Munchies

Call it a snack, a bite, a nibble or a nosh—some of the most satisfying flavors come in small portions. Choose from sweet dainties, such as Hershey®'s Easy Chocolate Cracker Snacks or Creamy Chocolate Dipped Strawberries. Satisfy a craving for spice with Red Hot Pepper Wings. And because pizza is America's favorite munchie, there are recipes for Picnic Pizza Biscuits, Pizza Dippin' Strips and more. With so many yummy options, the hardest part may be finding enough snack time to try them all.

Easy Cheesy Artichoke & Spinach Bread (page 252)

Pizza Dippin' Strips

    1 package (13.8 ounces) refrigerated pizza crust dough
   15 thin slices pepperoni
    1 cup shredded mozzarella cheese (about 4 ounces)
    1 jar (1 pound 10 ounces) RAGÚ® Organic Pasta Sauce, heated

Preheat oven to 400°F.

On greased baking sheet, roll pizza dough into 12×9-inch rectangle. Fold edges over to make ¾-inch crust. Bake 7 minutes.

Evenly top pizza crust with pepperoni, then cheese. Bake an additional 8 minutes or until cheese is melted. Let stand 2 minutes.

Cut pizza in half lengthwise, then into 1½-inch strips. Serve with Pasta Sauce, heated, for dipping.   *Makes 16 strips*

Prep Time: 10 minutes
Cook Time: 15 minutes

Easy Cheesy Artichoke & Spinach Bread

    1 can (14 ounces) artichoke hearts, drained and chopped
    1 package (10 ounces) frozen chopped spinach or chopped broccoli, thawed and
        squeezed dry
    1 cup HELLMANN'S® or BEST FOODS® Real Mayonnaise
    1 cup grated Parmesan cheese
    1 clove garlic, finely chopped or ¼ teaspoon LAWRY'S® Garlic Powder with Parsley
        (optional)
    1 loaf French or Italian bread (about 16 inches long), halved lengthwise

1. Preheat oven to 350°F.

2. In small bowl, combine all ingredients except bread; evenly spread on bread. Bake 12 minutes or until golden and heated through.   *Makes 8 servings*

Prep Time: 10 minutes
Cook Time: 12 minutes

Pizza Dippin' Strips

Maraschino-Lemonade Pops

1 (10-ounce) jar maraschino cherries
8 (3-ounce) paper cups
1 (12-ounce) can frozen pink lemonade concentrate, partly thawed
¼ cup water
8 popsicle sticks

Drain cherries, reserving juice. Place one whole cherry in each paper cup. Coarsely chop remaining cherries. Add chopped cherries, lemonade concentrate, water and reserved juice to container of blender or food processor; blend until smooth. Fill paper cups with equal amounts of cherry mixture. Freeze several hours or until very slushy. Place popsicle sticks in the center of each cup. Freeze 1 hour longer or until firm. To serve, peel off paper cups.   *Makes 8 servings*

Note: Serve immediately after peeling off paper cups—these pops melt very quickly.

Favorite recipe from **Cherry Marketing Institute**

Cheesy Quesadillas

½ pound ground beef
1 medium onion, chopped
¼ teaspoon salt
1 can (4½ ounces) chopped green chilies, drained
1 jar (1 pound 10 ounces) RAGÚ® Robusto!® Pasta Sauce
8 (6½-inch) flour tortillas
1 tablespoon olive oil
2 cups shredded Cheddar and/or mozzarella cheese (about 8 ounces)

1. Preheat oven to 400°F. In 12-inch skillet, brown ground beef with onion and salt over medium-high heat; drain. Stir in chilies and ½ cup Ragú Pasta Sauce; set aside.

2. Meanwhile, evenly brush one side of 4 tortillas with half of the olive oil. On cookie sheets, arrange tortillas, oil-side down. Evenly top with ½ of the cheese, beef filling, then remaining cheese. Top with remaining 4 tortillas, then brush tops with remaining oil.

3. Bake 10 minutes or until cheese is melted. To serve, cut each quesadilla into 4 wedges. Serve with remaining sauce, heated.   *Makes 4 servings*

Prep Time: 10 minutes
Cook Time: 15 minutes

Maraschino-Lemonade Pops

Bite Size Tacos

  1 pound ground beef
  1 package (1.25 ounces) taco seasoning mix
  2 cups *French's*® French Fried Onions
  ¼ cup chopped fresh cilantro
32 bite-size round tortilla chips
  ¾ cup sour cream
  1 cup shredded Cheddar cheese

1. Cook beef in nonstick skillet over medium-high heat 5 minutes or until browned; drain. Stir in taco seasoning mix, *¾ cup water, 1 cup* French Fried Onions and cilantro. Simmer 5 minutes or until flavors are blended, stirring often.

2. Preheat oven to 350°F. Arrange tortilla chips on foil-lined baking sheet. Top with beef mixture, sour cream, remaining onions and cheese.

3. Bake 5 minutes or until cheese is melted and onions are golden.

Makes 8 appetizer servings

Prep Time: 5 minutes
Cook Time: 15 minutes

Cocoa Nut Bundles

1 can (8 ounces) refrigerated quick crescent dinner rolls
2 tablespoons butter or margarine, softened
1 tablespoon granulated sugar
2 teaspoons HERSHEY'S Cocoa
¼ cup chopped nuts
  Powdered sugar (optional)

1. Heat oven to 375°F. Unroll dough on ungreased cookie sheet and separate to form 8 triangles.

2. Combine butter, granulated sugar and cocoa in small bowl. Add nuts; mix thoroughly. Divide chocolate mixture evenly among triangles, placing on wide end of triangle. Take dough on either side of mixture and pull up and over mixture, tucking ends under. Continue rolling dough toward opposite point.

3. Bake 9 to 10 minutes or until golden brown. Sprinkle with powdered sugar, if desired; serve warm.

Makes 8 rolls

Bite Size Tacos

Cinnamon Apple Chips

2 cups unsweetened apple juice
1 cinnamon stick
2 Washington Red Delicious apples

1. In large skillet or saucepan, combine apple juice and cinnamon stick; bring to a low boil while preparing apples.

2. With paring knife, slice off ½ inch from tops and bottoms of apples and discard (or eat). Stand apples on either cut end; cut crosswise into ⅛-inch-thick slices, rotating apple as necessary to cut even slices.

3. Drop slices into boiling juice; cook 4 to 5 minutes or until slices appear translucent and lightly golden. Meanwhile, preheat oven to 250°F.

4. With slotted spatula, remove apple slices from juice and pat dry. Arrange slices on wire racks, making sure none overlap. Place racks on middle shelf in oven; bake 30 to 40 minutes until slices are lightly browned and almost dry to touch. Let chips cool on racks completely before storing in airtight container.   *Makes about 40 chips*

Tip: There is no need to core apples because boiling in juice for several minutes softens core and removes seeds.

*Favorite recipe from **Washington Apple Commission***

Patchwork Popcorn Party Mix

3 quarts popped JOLLY TIME® Pop Corn
2 cups rice or wheat cereal squares
½ cup dried cranberries or dried tart cherries
1 cup coarsely chopped walnuts, toasted
3 tablespoons butter or margarine
½ teaspoon maple extract

Place popped popcorn, cereal, cranberries and walnuts in large bowl. Melt butter in small pan. Stir in maple extract. Pour over popcorn mixture; toss well.   *Makes about 3½ quarts*

Cinnamon Apple Chips

SPAM™ French Bread Pizza

1 onion, chopped
1 green bell pepper, chopped
1 cup sliced fresh mushrooms
1 tablespoon vegetable oil
1 (16-ounce) loaf French bread
1 (12-ounce) can SPAM® Classic, cubed
1 cup chunky-style spaghetti sauce
2 cups (8 ounces) shredded mozzarella cheese

Heat oven to 425°F. In large skillet, sauté vegetables in oil 3 to 4 minutes or until tender. Cut bread in half lengthwise. Remove soft center, leaving two bread shells. Spoon vegetables and SPAM® into bread shells. Spoon spaghetti sauce over SPAM®. Sprinkle with cheese. Place shells on baking sheet. Bake 10 to 15 minutes or until cheese is melted and bubbly.

Makes 8 servings

Creamy Chocolate Dipped Strawberries

1 cup HERSHEY¡'S Semi-Sweet Chocolate Chips
½ cup HERSHEY¡'S Premier White Chips
1 tablespoon shortening (do *not* use butter, margarine, spread or oil)
Fresh strawberries, rinsed and patted dry (about 2 pints)

1. Line tray with wax paper.

2. Place chocolate chips, white chips and shortening in medium microwave-safe bowl. Microwave at HIGH (100%) 1 minute; stir. If necessary, microwave at HIGH an additional 15 seconds at a time, stirring after each heating, just until chips are melted when stirred. Holding top, dip bottom two-thirds of each strawberry into melted mixture; shake gently to remove excess. Place on prepared tray.

3. Refrigerate about 1 hour or until coating is firm. Cover; refrigerate leftover dipped berries. For best results, use within 24 hours.   *Makes about 3 dozen dipped berries*

Tex-Mex Potato Skins

3 hot baked potatoes, split lengthwise
¾ cup (3 ounces) shredded Cheddar or pepper Jack cheese
1⅓ cups *French's* ® French Fried Onions, divided
¼ cup chopped green chilies
¼ cup crumbled cooked bacon
   Salsa and sour cream

1. Preheat oven to 350°F. Scoop out inside of potatoes, leaving ¼-inch shells. Reserve inside of potatoes for another use.

2. Arrange potato halves on baking sheet. Top with cheese, ⅔ *cup* French Fried Onions, chilies and bacon.

3. Bake 15 minutes or until heated through and cheese is melted. Cut each potato half crosswise into thirds. Serve topped with salsa, sour cream and remaining onions.

Makes 18 appetizer servings

Tip: To bake potatoes quickly, microwave at HIGH 10 to 12 minutes or until tender.

Variation: For added Cheddar flavor, substitute *French's* ® **Cheddar French Fried Onions** for the original flavor.

Prep Time: 15 minutes
Cook Time: 15 minutes

Reese's® Haystacks

1⅔ cups (10-ounce package) REESE'S® Peanut Butter Chips
1 tablespoon shortening (do *not* use butter, margarine, spread or oil)
2½ cups (5-ounce can) chow mein noodles

1. Line tray with wax paper.

2. Place peanut butter chips and shortening in medium microwave-safe bowl. Microwave at HIGH (100%) 1 minute; stir. If necessary, microwave at HIGH an additional 15 seconds at a time, stirring after each heating, just until chips are melted and mixture is smooth when stirred. Immediately add chow mein noodles; stir to coat.

3. Drop mixture by heaping teaspoons onto prepared tray or into paper candy cups. Let stand until firm. If necessary, cover and refrigerate several minutes until firm. Store in tightly covered container.
Makes about 2 dozen treats

Picnic Pizza Biscuits

1 can (10 ounces) refrigerated buttermilk biscuits
1 pound hot Italian sausage, casings removed
½ cup chopped onion
½ cup sliced mushrooms
½ cup chopped green bell pepper
½ cup (2 ounces) shredded mozzarella cheese
¼ cup marinara or pizza sauce
2 tablespoons *French's*® Honey Dijon Mustard

1. Preheat oven to 375°F. Separate biscuits; pat or roll into 10 (4-inch) circles on floured surface. Press circles into 12-cup muffin pan.

2. Cook sausage in large nonstick skillet over high heat 5 minutes or until browned, stirring to separate meat; drain fat. Add onion, mushrooms and bell pepper; cook and stir 3 minutes or until vegetables are tender. Stir in cheese, sauce and mustard; mix well.

3. Mound filling evenly in biscuits. Bake 20 minutes or until biscuits are browned. Serve warm or at room temperature.
Makes 10 servings

Prep Time: 30 minutes
Cook Time: 25 minutes

Watermelon Kebobs

6 ounces (1-inch cubes) fat free turkey breast
6 ounces (1-inch cubes) reduced fat Cheddar cheese
18 cubes (1-inch) seedless watermelon
6 (6-inch) bamboo skewers

Alternate cubes of watermelon between cubes of turkey and cheese threaded onto each skewer, as shown.   *Makes 6 servings*

*Favorite recipe from **National Watermelon Promotion Board***

Original Ranch® Snack Mix

8 cups KELLOGG'S® CRISPIX®* cereal
2½ cups small pretzels
2½ cups bite-size Cheddar cheese crackers (optional)
3 tablespoons vegetable oil
1 packet (1 ounce) HIDDEN VALLEY® The Original Ranch® Salad Dressing & Seasoning Mix

*Kellogg's® and Crispix® are registered trademarks of Kellogg Company.

Combine cereal, pretzels and crackers in a gallon-size Glad® Zipper Storage Bag. Pour oil over mixture. Seal bag and toss to coat. Add salad dressing & seasoning mix; seal bag and toss again until coated.   *Makes 10 cups mix*

Watermelon Kebobs

Red Hot Pepper Wings

28 chicken wing drumettes (2¼ to 3 pounds)
2 tablespoons olive oil
    Salt and black pepper
¼ to ½ cup hot pepper sauce
2 tablespoons melted butter
1 teaspoon sugar

Brush chicken with oil; sprinkle with salt and pepper. Grill chicken on covered grill over medium KINGSFORD® Briquets about 20 minutes until juices run clear, turning every 5 minutes. Combine pepper sauce, butter and sugar in large bowl; add chicken and toss to coat. Serve hot or cold.

Makes 7 servings

Fiesta Chicken Nachos

1 tablespoon olive oil
1 pound boneless, skinless chicken breasts
1 jar (1 pound) RAGÚ® Cheesy! Double Cheddar Sauce
1 bag (9 ounces) tortilla chips
2 green and/or red bell peppers, diced
1 small onion, chopped
1 large tomato, diced

In 12-inch skillet, heat olive oil over medium-high heat and cook chicken, turning occasionally, 8 minutes or until thoroughly cooked. Remove from skillet; cut into strips.

In same skillet, combine chicken and Ragú Cheesy! Double Cheddar Sauce; heat through.

On serving platter, arrange layer of tortilla chips, then ½ of the sauce mixture, bell peppers, onion and tomato; repeat, ending with tomato. Garnish, if desired, with chopped fresh cilantro and shredded lettuce.

Makes 4 servings

Recipe Tip: For a spicier dish, add chopped jalapeño peppers or hot pepper sauce.

Red Hot Pepper Wings

Southwest-Spiced Walnuts

2 cups California walnuts
1 tablespoon sugar
1 teaspoon sea salt
½ teaspoon garlic powder
½ teaspoon ground cumin
¼ teaspoon cayenne pepper
1 tablespoon walnut oil

Preheat oven to 375°F. Plunge walnuts into a pot of boiling water, turn off heat and let stand 2 minutes; drain. Spread walnuts on baking sheet and roast 10 minutes. Measure seasonings in a small bowl and stir to combine. Heat oil in a skillet. Add walnuts and toss 1 minute. Add seasoning mixture and toss until walnuts are well coated. Cool on a paper towel.

Makes 2 cups

Favorite recipe from **Walnut Marketing Board**

Indian-Spiced Walnuts

2 egg whites, lightly beaten
1 tablespoon ground cumin
1½ teaspoons curry powder
1½ teaspoons salt
½ teaspoon sugar
4 cups California walnuts, halves and pieces

Preheat oven to 350°F. Coat large, shallow baking pan with nonstick cooking spray. In large bowl, mix egg whites with spices, salt and sugar. Stir in walnuts and coat thoroughly. Spread in prepared pan. Bake 15 to 18 minutes or until dry and crisp. Cool completely before serving.

Makes 4 cups

Favorite recipe from **Walnut Marketing Board**

Southwest-Spiced Walnuts and Indian-Spiced Walnuts

Coconut Honey Popcorn Balls

    3 quarts popped JOLLY TIME® Pop Corn
    ¾ cup coconut
    ⅓ cup honey
    ½ teaspoon ground cinnamon
        Dash of salt
    3 tablespoons butter or margarine

Preheat oven to 250°F. Line shallow pan with foil. Place popped popcorn in pan. Keep popcorn warm in oven. Spread coconut in shallow baking pan; toast coconut, stirring once, about 8 to 10 minutes. Combine honey, cinnamon and salt in small saucepan. Heat to boiling; boil 2½ minutes, stirring constantly. Add butter; stir until melted. Pour honey mixture over popcorn. Add coconut. Toss well. Cool just enough to handle. With JOLLY TIME® Pop Corn Ball Maker or buttered hands, shape into balls.

Makes about 10 popcorn balls

Veggie Pizza Cupcakes

    1 package (12 ounces) refrigerated biscuits (10 biscuits)
    1 teaspoon olive oil
    1½ cups assorted diced fresh vegetables (red bell pepper, zucchini, summer squash, onion)
    1½ cups (14 ounces) RAGÚ® Organic Pasta or Old World Style ® Pasta Sauce
    ½ cup shredded mozzarella cheese (about 2 ounces)

1. Preheat oven to 375°F. Unroll biscuits and press each into a 3-inch round. In 12-cup muffin pan, evenly press 1 biscuit on bottom and up side of each cup; chill until ready to fill.

2. In 10-inch skillet, heat olive oil over medium heat and cook vegetables, stirring occasionally, 5 minutes or until tender. Stir in Pasta Sauce and bring to a boil over high heat. Reduce heat to low and simmer 2 minutes or until slightly reduced.

3. Evenly spoon vegetable mixture into prepared muffin cups. Bake 15 minutes. Evenly sprinkle tops with cheese and bake an additional 5 minutes or until cheese is melted and biscuits are golden. Let stand 5 minutes before serving. Gently remove pizza cups from muffin pan and serve.

Makes 10 pizza cups

Prep Time: 10 minutes
Cook Time: 25 minutes

*Patchwork Popcorn Party Mix (page 258) and
Coconut Honey Popcorn Balls*

Hidden Valley® Torta

2 packages (8 ounces each) cream cheese, softened
1 packet (1 ounce) HIDDEN VALLEY® The Original Ranch® Salad Dressing & Seasoning Mix
1 jar (6 ounces) marinated artichoke hearts, drained and chopped
⅓ cup roasted red peppers, drained and chopped
3 tablespoons minced fresh parsley

Beat cream cheese and salad dressing & seasoning mix together in a medium bowl. In a separate bowl, stir together artichokes, peppers and parsley. In a 3-cup bowl lined with plastic wrap, alternate layers of cream cheese mixture and vegetable mixture, beginning and ending with a cheese layer.

Chill 4 hours or overnight. Invert onto plate; remove plastic wrap. Serve with crackers.

Makes 10 to 12 servings

Cheddar Cheese and Rice Roll

2 cups cooked UNCLE BEN'S® ORIGINAL CONVERTED® Brand Rice
3 cups grated low-fat Cheddar cheese
¾ cup fat-free cream cheese, softened
1 can (4½ ounces) green chilies, drained, chopped
⅛ teaspoon hot sauce
1½ cups chopped walnuts

PREP: CLEAN: Wash hands. Combine rice, Cheddar cheese, cream cheese, chilies and hot sauce. Mix by hand or in food processor. Shape mixture into a log. Roll in walnuts. Wrap tightly with plastic wrap and refrigerate 1 hour.

SERVE: Serve with assorted crackers.

CHILL: Refrigerate leftovers immediately.

Makes 15 servings

Prep Time: 20 minutes
Cook Time: none
Chill Time: 1 hour

Hidden Valley® Torta

Nachos à la Ortega®

    1 can (16 ounces) ORTEGA® Refried Beans, warmed
    4 cups baked tortilla chips
    1½ cups (6 ounces) shredded Monterey Jack cheese
    2 tablespoons ORTEGA Jalapeños, sliced

Suggested Toppings
    ORTEGA Salsa-Thick & Chunky, sour cream, guacamole, sliced ripe olives, chopped green onions, chopped fresh cilantro (optional)

PREHEAT broiler.

SPREAD beans over bottom of large ovenproof platter or 15×10-inch jelly-roll pan. Arrange chips over beans. Top with cheese and jalapeños.

BROIL for 1 to 1½ minutes or until cheese is melted. Top with desired toppings.

Makes 4 to 6 servings

Confetti Tuna in Celery Sticks

    1 (3-ounce) STARKIST Flavor Fresh Pouch® Tuna (Albacore or Chunk Light)
    ½ cup shredded red or green cabbage
    ½ cup shredded carrots
    ¼ cup shredded yellow squash or zucchini
    3 tablespoons reduced-calorie cream cheese, softened
    1 tablespoon plain low-fat yogurt
    ½ teaspoon dried basil, crushed
    Salt and pepper to taste
    10 to 12 (4-inch) celery sticks, with leaves if desired

In a small bowl toss together tuna, cabbage, carrots and squash.

Stir in cream cheese, yogurt and basil. Add salt and pepper to taste.

With small spatula spread mixture evenly into celery sticks.

Makes 10 servings

Prep Time: 20 minutes

Nachos à la Ortega®

Hershey's Easy Chocolate Cracker Snacks

1⅔ cups (10-ounce package) HERSHEY'S Mint Chocolate Chips*
2 cups (12-ounce package) HERSHEY'S Semi-Sweet Chocolate Chips
2 tablespoons shortening (do not use butter, margarine, spread or oil)
60 to 70 round buttery crackers (about one-half 1-pound box)

*2 cups (11.5-ounce package) HERSHEY'S Milk Chocolate Chips and ¼ teaspoon pure peppermint extract can be substituted for mint chocolate chips.

1. Line several trays or cookie sheets with wax paper.

2. Place mint chocolate chips, chocolate chips and shortening in large microwave-safe bowl. Microwave at HIGH (100%) 1 minute; stir. Continue heating 30 seconds at a time, stirring after each heating, until chips are melted and mixture is smooth when stirred.

3. Drop crackers into chocolate mixture one at a time. Using tongs, push cracker into chocolate so that it is covered completely. (If chocolate begins to thicken, reheat 10 to 20 seconds in microwave.) Remove from chocolate, tapping lightly on edge of bowl to remove excess chocolate. Place on prepared tray. Refrigerate until chocolate hardens, about 20 minutes. For best results, store tightly covered in refrigerator. *Makes about 5½ dozen crackers*

Peanut Butter and Milk Chocolate: Use 1⅔ cups (10-ounce package) REESE'S® Peanut Butter Chips, 2 cups (11.5-ounce package) HERSHEY'S Milk Chocolate Chips and 2 tablespoons shortening. Proceed as directed.

White Chip and Toffee: Melt 2 bags (12 ounces each) HERSHEY'S Premier White Chips and 2 tablespoons shortening. Dip crackers; before coating hardens sprinkle with HEATH® BITS 'O BRICKLE® Toffee Bits.

Bread & Muffins

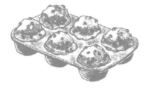

Nothing makes a house feel more like home than the aroma of fresh baked bread or muffins. Watching dough rise is almost magical and is there anything on earth more wonderful than the first bite of a Homemade Cinnamon Roll? You'll find recipes here for yeast breads, quick breads, muffins and scones. Bake the perfect Pumpkin-Nut Bread and start a holiday tradition. Delight the kids with Peanut Butter Mini Muffins topped with "M&Ms".® Whatever you bake will warm hearts as well as your kitchen.

Hot Rolls (page 304)

Apricot-Peanut Butter Muffins

1¾ cups PILLSBURY BEST® All-Purpose or Unbleached Flour
2½ tablespoons sugar
2½ teaspoons baking powder
¾ teaspoon salt
¼ cup CRISCO® Shortening plus additional for greasing
¼ cup JIF® Creamy Peanut Butter
¾ cup milk
2 eggs
2 tablespoons SMUCKER'S® Apricot Preserves

1. Preheat oven to 400°F. Grease 10 large muffin pan cups.

2. Combine flour, sugar, baking powder and salt in large bowl; cut in ¼ cup CRISCO Shortening and peanut butter with pastry blender or 2 knives.

3. Combine milk and eggs in small bowl; add all at once to dry ingredients. Stir just until dry ingredients are moistened.

4. Fill muffin cups ⅔ full. Spoon about ½ teaspoon preserves into center of each muffin.

5. Bake at 400°F for 25 minutes or until toothpick inserted near centers comes out clean.

Makes 10 muffins

Variation: Substitute your favorite SMUCKER'S® flavor in place of the apricot preserves in the above recipe. Experiment with strawberry or blackberry preserves or even apple butter.

Pumpkin-Nut Bread

4½ to 4¾ cups all-purpose flour, divided
⅓ cup firmly packed brown sugar
2 envelopes FLEISCHMANN'S® RapidRise™ Yeast
1½ teaspoons salt
½ cup evaporated milk
¼ cup butter or margarine
1 cup canned pumpkin
2 large eggs
⅔ cup finely chopped pecans or walnuts, toasted
1½ teaspoons pumpkin pie spice
1 egg white
1 tablespoon water

In large bowl, combine 1½ cups flour, sugar, undissolved yeast and salt. Heat milk and butter until very warm (120° to 130°F); stir into dry ingredients. Beat 2 minutes at medium speed of electric mixer, scraping bowl occasionally. Stir in pumpkin, eggs and 1 cup flour. Beat 2 minutes at high speed. Stir in nuts, pumpkin pie spice and enough remaining flour to make soft dough. Knead on lightly floured surface until smooth and elastic, about 8 to 10 minutes. Cover; let rest 10 minutes.

Divide dough in half; roll each half to 12×7-inch rectangle. Roll up tightly from short end as for jelly roll; pinch to seal. Place, seam sides down, in 2 greased 8½×4½-inch loaf pans.

Cover; let rise until doubled in size, about 1 hour. Brush with egg white mixed with 1 tablespoon water. Bake at 350°F for 25 to 30 minutes or until loaves sound hollow when tapped. Remove from pans and cool on wire rack.

Makes 2 loaves

Honey Roasted Ham Biscuits

1 (10-ounce) can refrigerated buttermilk biscuits
2 cups (12 ounces) diced HORMEL® CURE81® ham
½ cup honey mustard
¼ cup finely chopped honey roasted peanuts, divided

Heat oven to 400°F. Separate biscuits. Place in muffin pan cups, pressing gently into bottoms and up sides of cups. In bowl, combine ham, honey mustard and 2 tablespoons peanuts. Spoon ham mixture evenly into biscuit cups. Sprinkle with remaining 2 tablespoons peanuts. Bake 15 to 17 minutes.

Makes 10 servings

Morning Glory Bread

2½ cups all-purpose flour
2 teaspoons baking powder
1 teaspoon baking soda
½ teaspoon salt
½ teaspoon ground cinnamon
¼ teaspoon *each* ground nutmeg and ground allspice
¾ cup granulated sugar
¾ cup firmly packed light brown sugar
½ cup MOTT'S® Chunky Apple Sauce
3 egg whites
1 tablespoon vegetable oil
1 tablespoon GRANDMA'S® Molasses
¾ cup finely shredded carrots
½ cup raisins
⅓ cup drained crushed pineapple in juice
¼ cup shredded coconut

1. Preheat oven to 375°F. Spray 8½×4½-inch loaf pan with nonstick cooking spray.

2. In large bowl, combine flour, baking powder, baking soda, salt, cinnamon, nutmeg and allspice.

3. In medium bowl, combine granulated sugar, brown sugar, apple sauce, egg whites, oil and molasses.

4. Stir apple sauce mixture into flour mixture just until moistened. Fold in carrots, raisins, pineapple and coconut. Spread into prepared pan.

5. Bake 45 to 50 minutes or until toothpick inserted in center comes out clean. Cool in pan 10 minutes. Invert onto wire rack; turn right side up. Cool completely. Cut into 16 slices.

Makes 16 servings

Honey Roasted Ham Biscuits

Mexican Bubble Rolls

    2 cups warm water (100°F to 110°F)
    2 envelopes FLEISCHMANN'S® Active Dry Yeast
    ¼ cup sugar
    ¼ cup butter or margarine, softened
    1 tablespoon salt
    4 to 4½ cups all-purpose flour
 1½ cups yellow cornmeal
    2 jars (4 ounces each) diced pimientos, well-drained
    ¾ cup grated Parmesan cheese
    1 tablespoon whole cumin seed, toasted

Place ½ cup warm water in large warm bowl. Sprinkle in yeast; stir until dissolved. Add remaining water, sugar, butter, salt, 1½ cups flour and cornmeal; blend well. Beat 2 minutes at medium speed of electric mixer, scraping bowl occasionally. Add 1 cup flour; beat 2 minutes at high speed. Stir in enough remaining flour to make soft dough. Knead on floured surface until smooth, about 8 to 10 minutes. Place in greased bowl, turning to grease top. Cover; let rise in warm, draft-free place until doubled in size, about 1 hour.

Meanwhile, combine pimientos, cheese and cumin seed in small bowl. Mix well. Punch dough down. On floured surface, divide dough into 24 pieces; flatten to 3-inch circles. Place 2 teaspoons pimiento mixture in center of each circle. Pull up dough to enclose filling and pinch to seal. Place balls, sealed side down, in 2 greased 9-inch round cake pans.* Cover; let rise in warm, draft-free place until doubled in size, about 30 minutes. Bake at 375°F for 25 minutes or until done. Remove from pans; cool on wire racks. *Makes 24 rolls*

Two 10-cup tube pans may be used. Bake at 375°F for 30 minutes or until done.

Quick Corn Bread with Chilies 'n' Cheese

   1 package (12 to 16 ounces) corn bread or corn muffin mix
   1 cup (4 ounces) shredded Monterey Jack cheese, divided
   1 can (4 ounces) chopped green chilies, drained
   1 envelope LIPTON® RECIPE SECRETS® Vegetable Soup Mix

Prepare corn bread mix according to package directions; stir in ½ cup cheese, chilies and vegetable soup mix. Pour batter into lightly greased 8-inch baking pan; bake as directed. While warm, top with remaining ½ cup cheese. Cool completely on wire rack. To serve, cut into squares. *Makes 16 servings*

Honey of a Whole Wheat Bread

1-Pound Loaf
   ¼ cup water
   ¼ cup milk
   1 large egg, at room temperature
   2 tablespoons honey
   2 teaspoons butter, cut into small pieces
   1½ teaspoons salt
   ⅔ cup whole wheat flour
   1⅓ cups bread flour
   1½ teaspoons RED STAR® Active Dry Yeast or 1 teaspoon QUICK•RISE™ Yeast or Bread Machine Yeast

1½-Pound Loaf
   ¼ cup water
   ½ cup milk
   1 large egg, at room temperature
   ¼ cup honey
   1 tablespoon butter, cut into small pieces
   2 teaspoons salt
   1 cup whole wheat flour
   2 cups bread flour
   2¼ teaspoons (1 packet) RED STAR® Active Dry Yeast or 1½ teaspoons QUICK•RISE™ Yeast or Bread Machine Yeast

Bread Machine Directions

Place room temperature ingredients in pan in order listed. Select basic/white cycle, medium crust. Do not use delay timer. Check dough consistency after 5 minutes of kneading making adjustments, if necessary. Cool on rack. *Makes 1 loaf*

Quick Corn Bread with Chilies 'n' Cheese

Peanut Butter Mini Muffins

⅓ **cup creamy peanut butter**
¼ **cup (½ stick) butter, softened**
¼ **cup granulated sugar**
¼ **cup firmly packed light brown sugar**
 1 **large egg**
¾ **cup buttermilk**
 3 **tablespoons vegetable oil**
¾ **teaspoon vanilla extract**
1½ **cups all-purpose flour**
¾ **teaspoon baking powder**
½ **teaspoon baking soda**
½ **teaspoon salt**
1¼ **cups "M&M's"® Milk Chocolate Mini Baking Bits, divided**
    Chocolate Glaze (recipe follows)

Preheat oven to 350°F. Lightly grease 36 (1¾-inch) mini muffin cups or line with paper or foil liners; set aside. In large bowl cream peanut butter, butter and sugars until light and fluffy; beat in egg. Beat in buttermilk, oil and vanilla. In medium bowl combine flour, baking powder, baking soda and salt; gradually blend into creamed mixture. Divide batter evenly among prepared muffin cups. Sprinkle batter evenly with ¾ cup "M&M's"® Milk Chocolate Mini Baking Bits. Bake 15 to 17 minutes or until toothpick inserted in centers comes out clean. Cool completely on wire racks. Prepare Chocolate Glaze. Place glaze in resealable plastic sandwich bag; seal bag. Cut tiny piece off one corner of bag (not more than ⅛ inch). Drizzle glaze over muffins. Decorate with remaining ½ cup "M&M's"® Milk Chocolate Mini Baking Bits; let glaze set. Store in tightly covered container. *Makes 3 dozen mini muffins*

Chocolate Glaze: In top of double boiler over hot water melt 2 (1-ounce) squares semi-sweet chocolate and 1 tablespoon butter. Stir until smooth; let cool slightly.

Peanut Butter Mini Muffins

Homemade Cinnamon Rolls

4¼ to 4¾ cups all-purpose flour, divided
1 package quick-rising active dry yeast
1¼ cups plus 4 to 5 teaspoons milk, divided
¼ cup granulated sugar
¼ cup (½ stick) plus 6 tablespoons butter, softened, divided
2 teaspoons WATKINS® Vanilla, divided
5 teaspoons WATKINS® Ground Cinnamon, divided
1 teaspoon salt
2 eggs
½ cup packed brown sugar
1 cup powdered sugar

Combine 1½ cups flour and yeast in large bowl. Heat 1¼ cups milk, granulated sugar, ¼ cup butter, 1 teaspoon vanilla, 1 teaspoon cinnamon and salt just until mixture is warm (120° to 130°F), stirring constantly. Add to flour mixture with eggs; beat with electric mixer at low speed for 30 seconds, scraping side of bowl frequently. Beat at high speed for 3 minutes.

Stir in as much remaining flour as possible with spoon (dough will be soft). Knead in enough remaining flour to form moderately soft dough, 3 to 5 minutes total. Shape dough into a ball; place in lightly greased bowl, turning once. Cover and let rise in warm place for about 1 to 1½ hours until doubled in size. (Dough is ready to shape when you can lightly press two fingers ½ inch into dough and indentation remains.) Punch down dough and divide in half. Place each half on lightly floured surface and smooth into a ball. Cover and let rest 10 minutes.

Preheat oven to 350°F. Grease 13×9-inch baking pan. Roll half of dough into 12×8-inch rectangle on lightly floured surface. Spread with 3 tablespoons butter. Combine brown sugar and remaining 4 teaspoons cinnamon; sprinkle half of mixture over rectangle. Roll up dough from short side; seal edges by brushing with water. Repeat with remaining dough. Slice one roll into 8 pieces and other into 7 pieces. Arrange slices cut sides up in prepared pan. Cover and let rise for about 30 minutes or until nearly doubled.

Bake for 25 to 40 minutes or until light brown. Immediately invert rolls onto wire rack, then turn right side up. Cool slightly on wire rack. Combine powdered sugar, remaining 4 teaspoons milk and 1 teaspoon vanilla in small bowl until smooth; drizzle glaze over rolls. Serve warm or store in airtight container.

Makes 15 rolls

Homemade Cinnamon Rolls

Gingerbread Streusel Raisin Muffins

1 cup raisins
½ cup boiling water
⅓ cup margarine or butter, softened
¾ cup GRANDMA'S® Molasses (Unsulphured)
1 egg
2 cups all-purpose flour
1½ teaspoons baking soda
1 teaspoon ground cinnamon
1 teaspoon ground ginger
½ teaspoon salt

Topping
⅓ cup all-purpose flour
¼ cup firmly packed brown sugar
¼ cup chopped nuts
3 tablespoons margarine or butter
1 teaspoon cinnamon

Preheat oven to 375°F. Grease bottoms only of 12 muffin cups or line with paper baking cups. In small bowl, cover raisins with boiling water; let stand 5 minutes. In large bowl, beat ⅓ cup margarine and molasses until fluffy. Add egg; beat well. Stir in 2 cups flour, baking soda, 1 teaspoon cinnamon, ginger and salt. Blend just until dry ingredients are moistened. Gently stir in raisins and water. Fill prepared muffin cups ¾ full. For topping, combine all ingredients in small bowl. Sprinkle over muffins.

Bake 20 to 25 minutes or until toothpick inserted in centers comes out clean. Cool 5 minutes; remove from pan. Serve warm. *Makes 12 muffins*

Donna's Heavenly Orange Chip Scones

4 cups all-purpose flour
1 cup granulated sugar
4 teaspoons baking powder
½ teaspoon baking soda
½ teaspoon salt
1 cup (6 ounces) NESTLÉ® TOLL HOUSE® Semi-Sweet Chocolate Mini Morsels
1 cup golden raisins
1 tablespoon grated orange peel
1 cup (2 sticks) unsalted butter, cut into pieces and softened
1 cup buttermilk
3 large eggs, *divided*
1 teaspoon orange extract
1 tablespoon milk
Icing (recipe follows)

PREHEAT oven to 350°F. Lightly grease baking sheets.

COMBINE flour, granulated sugar, baking powder, baking soda and salt in large bowl. Add morsels, raisins and orange peel; mix well. Cut in butter with pastry blender or two knives until mixture resembles coarse crumbs. Combine buttermilk, *2 eggs* and orange extract in small bowl. Pour buttermilk mixture into flour mixture; mix just until a sticky dough is formed. Do not overmix. Drop by level ¼-cup measure onto prepared baking sheets. Combine *remaining* egg and milk in small bowl. Brush egg mixture over top of dough.

BAKE for 18 to 22 minutes or until wooden pick inserted in center comes out clean. For best results, bake one baking sheet at a time. Cool on wire racks for 10 minutes. Drizzle scones with icing. Serve warm.

Makes 2 dozen scones

Icing: **COMBINE** 2 cups powdered sugar, ¼ cup orange juice, 1 tablespoon grated orange peel and 1 teaspoon orange extract in medium bowl. Mix until smooth.

Donna's Heavenly Orange Chip Scones

Peachy Oat Bran Muffins

1½ cups oat bran
½ cup all-purpose flour
⅓ cup firmly packed brown sugar
2 teaspoons baking powder
1 teaspoon cinnamon
½ teaspoon salt
¾ cup lowfat milk
1 egg, beaten
¼ cup vegetable oil
1 can (15 ounces) DEL MONTE® LITE® Yellow Cling Sliced Peaches, drained and chopped
⅓ cup chopped walnuts
Granulated sugar (optional)

1. Preheat oven to 425°F. Combine oat bran, flour, brown sugar, baking powder, cinnamon and salt; mix well.

2. Combine milk, egg and oil. Add to dry ingredients; stir just enough to blend. Fold in fruit and nuts.

3. Fill greased muffin cups with batter. Sprinkle with granulated sugar, if desired.

4. Bake 20 to 25 minutes or until golden brown.   *Makes 12 medium muffins*

Hint: Muffins can be frozen and reheated in a microwave or toaster oven.

Prep Time: 10 minutes
Bake Time: 25 minutes

Peachy Oat Bran Muffins

Crispy Onion Flat Breads

2½ cups all-purpose baking mix
2 cups *French's*® French Fried Onions, divided
1 cup shredded Cheddar cheese
¼ cup grated Parmesan cheese
½ cup water
2 tablespoons *Frank's*® RedHot® Original Cayenne Pepper Sauce
1 egg white, beaten

1. Combine baking mix, ⅔ *cup* French Fried Onions and cheeses in large bowl. Stir in water and *Frank's RedHot* Sauce until mixture is blended (dough will be sticky). With hands, knead dough until it comes together and forms a ball. Press into 6-inch square and divide into 24 equal pieces; cover with plastic wrap.

2. Move 2 oven racks to lowest positions. Preheat oven to 325°F. Crush remaining onions. Roll each piece of dough to ¹⁄₁₆-inch thickness on well-floured surface. Place on parchment-lined or ungreased baking sheets. Brush dough with egg white; sprinkle with about 1 tablespoon crushed onions. Prick dough with fork several times.

3. Bake 15 to 17 minutes or until golden, rotating baking sheets from top to bottom. Cool flat breads on baking sheets for 1 minute. Transfer to cooling rack; cool completely. Flat breads may be stored in airtight container for up to 1 week.   *Makes 2 dozen flat breads*

Prep Time: 20 minutes
Cook Time: 17 minutes

Grandma's® Bran Muffins

2½ cups bran flakes, divided
1 cup raisins
1 cup boiling water
2 cups buttermilk
1 cup GRANDMA'S® Molasses
½ cup canola oil
2 eggs, beaten
2¾ cups all-purpose flour
2½ teaspoons baking soda
½ teaspoon salt

Heat oven to 400°F. In medium bowl, mix 1 cup bran flakes, raisins and water. Set aside. In large bowl, combine remaining ingredients. Stir in bran-raisin mixture. Pour into greased muffin pan cups. Fill ⅔ full and bake for 20 minutes. Remove muffins and place on rack to cool.

Makes 48 muffins

Hot Rolls

6 cups sifted PILLSBURY BEST® All-Purpose or Unbleached Flour
½ cup sugar
1 teaspoon salt
1 egg
¾ CRISCO® Butter Flavor Stick or ¾ cup CRISCO® Butter Flavor Shortening
2 packages dry yeast
2 cups lukewarm water
1 stick butter

1. Sift PILLSBURY BEST Flour, sugar and salt together; add egg and CRISCO Shortening. Dissolve yeast in 1 cup water; add to mixture. Add remaining 1 cup water. Mix with hands for 5 minutes or until thoroughly mixed. Cover with waxed paper and refrigerate overnight.

2. Melt butter. Roll out dough to ½-inch thickness on floured board; cut with 2½-inch biscuit cutter. Dip in melted butter and fold over, pressing lightly. Place on ungreased baking sheet; let rise 1 to 2 hours.

3. Preheat oven to 400°F. Bake rolls 10 minutes.

Makes 3 dozen rolls

Prep Time: 10 minutes
Chill Time: overnight
Rise Time: 1 to 2 hours
Bake Time: 10 minutes

Grandma's® Bran Muffins

Ragin' Cornbread

   1 egg
   ¼ CRISCO® Stick or ¼ cup CRISCO® Shortening, melted
1⅓ cups milk
   2 cups MARTHA WHITE® Self-Rising Corn Meal Mix
   1 can (4½ ounces) chopped green chiles
   2 cups shredded sharp Cheddar cheese
   ½ pound hot bulk pork sausage, browned and drained
   2 to 4 tablespoons chopped pickled jalapeño pepper
   ¼ teaspoon hot pepper sauce

Preheat oven to 450°F. Grease 10½-inch cast iron skillet with CRISCO Shortening and place in oven to heat. Beat egg in large bowl. Add melted shortening, milk and MARTHA WHITE® Corn Meal Mix; blend well. Stir in remaining ingredients; mix well. Pour into hot skillet. Bake 20 to 25 minutes or until golden brown. Turn out onto serving plate; cut into wedges and serve.   *Makes 10 servings*

Golden Apple Buttermilk Bread

1½ cups unsifted all-purpose flour
   1 cup whole wheat flour
   ½ cup natural bran cereal
   1 teaspoon baking soda
   ½ teaspoon baking powder
   ¼ teaspoon ground ginger
1⅓ cups buttermilk
   ¾ cup sugar
   ¼ cup vegetable oil
   1 large egg
   1 teaspoon grated orange peel
   1 cup chopped Washington Golden Delicious apples

1. Heat oven to 350°F. Grease 9×5-inch loaf pan. In medium bowl, combine flours, cereal, baking soda, baking powder and ginger. In large bowl, beat together buttermilk, sugar, oil, egg and orange peel.

2. Add flour mixture to buttermilk mixture, stirring just until combined. Fold in apples. Spread batter in prepared pan and bake 45 to 50 minutes or until wooden toothpick inserted into center comes out clean. Cool bread in pan 10 minutes. Remove from pan and cool on wire rack.
   Makes 1 loaf (8 servings)

*Favorite recipe from **Washington Apple Commission***

Ragin' Cornbread

Lemon Poppy Seed Tea Loaf

Tea Loaf

2½ cups all-purpose flour

¼ cup poppy seeds

1 tablespoon grated lemon peel

2 teaspoons baking powder

½ teaspoon baking soda

½ teaspoon salt

1 cup sugar

⅔ cup MOTT'S® Natural Apple Sauce

1 whole egg

2 egg whites, lightly beaten

2 tablespoons vegetable oil

1 teaspoon vanilla extract

⅓ cup skim milk

Lemon Syrup

¼ cup sugar

¼ cup lemon juice

1. Preheat oven to 350°F. Spray 9×5-inch loaf pan with nonstick cooking spray.

2. To prepare Tea Loaf, in large bowl, combine flour, poppy seeds, lemon peel, baking powder, baking soda and salt.

3. In medium bowl, combine 1 cup sugar, apple sauce, whole egg, egg whites, oil and vanilla.

4. Stir apple sauce mixture into flour mixture alternately with milk. Mix until thoroughly moistened. Spread batter into prepared pan.

5. Bake 40 to 45 minutes or until toothpick inserted in center comes out clean. Cool in pan 10 minutes. Invert onto wire rack; turn right side up.

6. To prepare Lemon Syrup, in small saucepan, combine ¼ cup sugar and lemon juice. Cook, stirring frequently, until sugar dissolves. Cool slightly.

7. Pierce top of loaf in several places with metal skewer. Brush lemon syrup over loaf. Let stand until cool. Cut into 16 slices. *Makes 16 servings*

Left to right: Lemon Poppy Seed Tea Loaf and Morning Glory Bread (page 286)

Cakes & Pies

Nothing is more celebrated or better appreciated by family and friends than a homemade cake or pie, and these recipes are guaranteed to earn you plenty of "oohs" and "ahhs." Libby's® Famous Pumpkin Pie or Nestlé® Toll House® Chocolate Chip Pie will do any sweet table proud. For a birthday cake that will be devoured down to the last crumb, bake Banana Fudge Layer Cake or Fudgy Ripple Cake. Sweet dreams are made of nothing more than a few simple ingredients, a preheated oven and a little bit of your time.

Carnation® Key Lime Pie

1 *prepared* 9-inch (6 ounces) graham cracker crumb crust
1 can (14 ounces) NESTLÉ® CARNATION® Sweetened Condensed Milk
½ cup (about 3 medium limes) fresh lime juice
1 teaspoon grated lime peel
2 cups frozen whipped topping, thawed
    Lime peel twists or lime slices (optional)

BEAT sweetened condensed milk and lime juice in small mixer bowl until combined; stir in lime peel. Pour into crust; spread with whipped topping. Refrigerate for 2 hours or until set. Garnish with lime peel twists. *Makes 8 servings*

Blueberry Pie

6 cups fresh *or* 2 packages (16 ounces each) frozen unsweetened blueberries
3 tablespoons lemon juice
1 cup plus 2 tablespoons EQUAL® SPOONFUL*
6 tablespoons cornstarch
    Pastry for double-crust 9-inch pie

May substitute 27 packets EQUAL® sweetener.

• Toss blueberries and lemon juice in large bowl. Sprinkle with combined Equal® and cornstarch; toss to coat. (If frozen blueberries are used, let stand 30 minutes.)

• Roll half of pastry on lightly floured surface into circle 1 inch larger than inverted 9-inch pie pan. Ease pastry into pan; trim within 1 inch of edge of pan. Roll remaining pastry to ⅛-inch thickness; cut into 10 to 12 strips, ½ inch wide.

• Pour blueberry mixture into pastry. Arrange pastry strips over filling and weave into lattice design. Trim ends of lattice strips; fold edge of lower crust over ends of lattice strips. Seal and flute edge.

• Bake in preheated 400°F oven 55 to 60 minutes or until pastry is browned and filling is bubbly. Cover edge of crust with aluminum foil if browning too quickly. Cool on wire rack; refrigerate leftovers. *Makes 8 servings*

Carnation® Key Lime Pie

Country Crunch Rhubarb Pie

CRISCO® Classic Single Pie Crust (page 316)

Crunch Layer
1 cup chopped pecans
¼ cup PILLSBURY BEST® All-Purpose or Unbleached Flour
¼ cup quick-cooking oats (not instant or old-fashioned)
¼ cup firmly packed brown sugar
½ teaspoon cinnamon
¼ teaspoon nutmeg
¼ cup softened butter or margarine

Filling
1½ cups granulated sugar
¼ cup PILLSBURY BEST® All-Purpose or Unbleached Flour
2 tablespoons quick-cooking tapioca
½ teaspoon cinnamon
½ teaspoon nutmeg
3½ cups fresh or frozen cut rhubarb (¼- to ½-inch pieces)
1 tablespoon butter or margarine
2 eggs, lightly beaten
1 (16-ounce) can pitted red tart cherries packed in water, well drained

Prepare CRISCO Pie Crust; cool completely. Preheat oven to 350°F. For crunch layer, combine pecans, PILLSBURY BEST® Flour, oats, brown sugar, cinnamon, ¼ teaspoon nutmeg and ¼ cup butter in medium bowl. Spread on baking sheet. Bake for 10 minutes, stirring several times. Cool. Break into small pieces. Place ¼ of mixture in bottom of baked pie crust. Set aside remaining mixture.

For filling, combine granulated sugar, PILLSBURY BEST® Flour, tapioca, cinnamon, nutmeg, rhubarb and butter in large saucepan. Cook and stir on medium heat until rhubarb begins to soften. Remove from heat. Stir small amount of hot mixture slowly into eggs, mixing thoroughly. Return egg mixture to saucepan. Cook and stir until mixture starts to thicken. Add cherries. Cook and stir until thickened. Cool slightly. Pour over crunch layer. Top with remaining crunch mixture.

Bake for 10 minutes. Cool to room temperature before serving. Refrigerate leftover pie.

Makes 1 (9-inch) pie

Prep Time: 65 minutes
Bake Time: 10 minutes

Classic CRISCO® Pie Crust

Single Crust
1⅓ cups PILLSBURY BEST® All-Purpose or Unbleached Flour
½ teaspoon salt
½ CRISCO® Butter Flavor Stick or ½ cup CRISCO® Butter Flavor Shortening
3 tablespoons cold water

Double Crust
2 cups PILLSBURY BEST® All-Purpose or Unbleached Flour
1 teaspoon salt
¾ CRISCO® Butter Flavor Stick or ¾ cup CRISCO® Butter Flavor Shortening
5 tablespoons cold water

1 (9-inch) Deep Dish Double or 2 (10-inch) Double Crust
2⅔ cups PILLSBURY BEST® All-Purpose or Unbleached Flour
1 teaspoon salt
1 CRISCO® Butter Flavor Stick or 1 cup CRISCO® Butter Flavor Shortening
7 to 8 tablespoons cold water

Spoon flour into measuring cup and level. Mix flour and salt in medium bowl. Cut in CRISCO Shortening using pastry blender (or 2 knives) until all flour is blended in to form pea-size chunks. Sprinkle with water, 1 tablespoon at a time. Toss lightly with fork until dough forms a ball.

Divide dough in half if making double crust. Press between hands to form 1 or 2 (5- to 6-inch) pancakes. Lightly flour dough. Roll into circle.

For single crust, transfer dough to pie plate using rolling pin. Press dough to fit. Fold edge under. Flute.

For double crust, lightly flour each half of dough. Roll into circles. Transfer bottom crust to pie plate using rolling pin. Press dough to fit. Trim edge even with pie plate. Add desired filling to unbaked pie crust. Lift top crust onto filled pie. Trim to ½-inch beyond edge of pie plate. Fold top edge under bottom crust. Flute. Cut slits in top crust to allow steam to escape. Bake according to specific recipe instructions.

For single baked pie shell, preheat oven to 425°F. Thoroughly prick bottom and sides with fork (50 times) to prevent shrinking. Bake for 10 to 15 minutes or until lightly browned.

For recipe calling for unbaked pie shell, bake according to specific recipe instructions.

Kahlúa® Chocolate Decadence

½ cup butter
8 ounces (8 squares) semisweet baking chocolate, divided
3 extra large eggs
¾ cup granulated sugar
1¼ cups finely ground walnuts or pecans
2 tablespoons all-purpose flour
5 tablespoons KAHLÚA® Liqueur, divided
1 teaspoon vanilla
Sifted powdered sugar
Strawberries, chocolate nonpareil candy or coffee beans for garnish

Preheat oven to 325°F. In small saucepan over medium heat, or in microwave-safe bowl on HIGH (100% power), melt butter and 6 ounces chocolate, stirring until blended. Remove from heat; cool. In large bowl, beat eggs and granulated sugar at high speed of electric mixer about 3 minutes or until light and lemon colored. Stir together walnuts and flour; gradually beat into egg mixture.

Stir 3 tablespoons Kahlúa® and vanilla into cooled chocolate mixture; gradually beat into egg mixture until well combined. Pour batter into 9-inch springform pan. Bake 35 to 45 minutes or until top is set. Cool cake in pan.

Remove side of pan; place cake on serving plate. Sprinkle top with powdered sugar. Melt remaining 2 ounces chocolate as previously directed. Stir together melted chocolate and remaining 2 tablespoons Kahlúa®; drizzle over cake. Decorate with strawberries, if desired.

Makes 1 (9-inch) cake

Banana Fudge Layer Cake

  1 package DUNCAN HINES® Moist Deluxe® Yellow Cake Mix
1⅓ cups water
  3 eggs
⅓ cup vegetable oil
  1 cup mashed ripe bananas (about 3 medium)
  1 container DUNCAN HINES® Chocolate Frosting

1. Preheat oven to 350°F. Grease and flour two 9-inch round cake pans.

2. Combine cake mix, water, eggs and oil in large bowl. Beat at low speed with electric mixer until moistened. Beat at medium speed 2 minutes. Stir in bananas.

3. Pour into prepared pans. Bake at 350°F for 28 to 31 minutes or until toothpick inserted in center comes out clean. Cool in pans 15 minutes. Remove from pans; cool completely.

4. Fill and frost cake with frosting. Garnish as desired.   *Makes 12 to 16 servings*

Reese's® Peanut Butter & Hershey's Kisses® Pie

  About 42 HERSHEY'S KISSES® Brand Milk Chocolates, divided
  2 tablespoons milk
  1 packaged (8-inch) crumb crust (6 ounces)
  1 package (8 ounces) cream cheese, softened
¾ cup sugar
  1 cup REESE'S® Creamy or Crunchy Peanut Butter
  1 tub (8 ounces) frozen non-dairy whipped topping, thawed and divided

1. Remove wrappers from chocolates. Place 26 chocolates and milk in small microwave-safe bowl. Microwave on HIGH (100%) 1 minute or just until melted and smooth when stirred. Spread evenly on bottom of crust. Refrigerate about 30 minutes.

2. Beat cream cheese with electric mixer on medium speed in medium bowl until smooth; gradually beat in sugar, then peanut butter, beating well after each addition. Reserve ½ cup whipped topping; fold remaining whipped topping into peanut butter mixture. Spoon into crust over chocolate. Cover; refrigerate about 6 hours or until set.

3. Garnish with reserved whipped topping and remaining chocolates. Cover; refrigerate leftover pie.   *Makes 8 servings*

Banana Fudge Layer Cake

Libby's® Famous Pumpkin Pie

¾ **cup granulated sugar**
1 **teaspoon ground cinnamon**
½ **teaspoon salt**
½ **teaspoon ground ginger**
¼ **teaspoon ground cloves**
2 **large eggs**
1 **can (15 ounces) LIBBY'S® 100% Pure Pumpkin**
1 **can (12 fluid ounces) NESTLÉ® CARNATION® Evaporated Milk**
1 *unbaked* **9-inch (4-cup volume) deep-dish pie shell**
   Whipped cream

MIX sugar, cinnamon, salt, ginger and cloves in small bowl. Beat eggs in large bowl. Stir in pumpkin and sugar-spice mixture. Gradually stir in evaporated milk.

POUR into pie shell.

BAKE in preheated 425°F. oven for 15 minutes. Reduce temperature to 350°F.; bake for 40 to 50 minutes or until knife inserted near center comes out clean. Cool on wire rack for 2 hours. Serve immediately or refrigerate. Top with whipped cream before serving.   *Makes 8 servings*

Note: Do not freeze, as this will cause the crust to separate from the filling.

Tip: 1¾ teaspoons pumpkin pie spice may be substituted for the cinnamon, ginger and cloves; however, the taste will be slightly different.

For 2 shallow pies: Substitute two 9-inch (2-cup volume) pie shells. Bake in preheated 425°F. oven for 15 minutes. Reduce temperature to 350°F.; bake for 20 to 30 minutes or until pies test done.

Orange Glazed Pound Cake

   1 package DUNCAN HINES® Moist Deluxe® Butter Recipe Golden Cake Mix
   4 eggs
   1 cup sour cream
   ⅓ cup vegetable oil
   ¼ cup plus 1 to 2 tablespoons orange juice, divided
   2 tablespoons grated orange peel
   1 cup confectioners' sugar

1. Preheat oven to 375°F. Grease and flour 10-inch tube pan.

2. Combine cake mix, eggs, sour cream, oil, ¼ cup orange juice and orange peel in large bowl. Beat at medium speed with electric mixer for 2 minutes. Pour into prepared pan. Bake at 375°F for 45 to 50 minutes or until toothpick inserted near center comes out clean. Cool in pan 25 minutes. Invert onto cooling rack. Cool completely.

3. Combine sugar and remaining 1 to 2 tablespoons orange juice in small bowl; stir until smooth. Drizzle over cake. Garnish as desired.   *Makes 12 to 16 servings*

Fudgey Chocolate Cupcakes

   ¾ cup water
   ½ cup (1 stick) 60% vegetable oil spread, melted
   2 egg whites, slightly beaten
   1 teaspoon vanilla extract
2¼ cups HERSHEY'S Basic Cocoa Baking Mix (recipe follows)
   2 teaspoons powdered sugar
   2 teaspoons HERSHEY'S Cocoa (optional)

1. Heat oven to 350°F. Line 16 muffin cups (2½ inches in diameter) with foil or paper bake cups.

2. Stir together water, melted spread, egg whites and vanilla in large bowl. Add Basic Cocoa Baking Mix; beat on low speed of mixer until blended. Fill muffin cups ⅔ full with batter.

3. Bake 20 to 25 minutes or until wooden pick inserted into centers comes out clean. Remove from pans to wire racks. Cool completely. Sift powdered sugar over tops of cupcakes. If desired, partially cover part of each cupcake with paper cutout. Sift cocoa over exposed powdered sugar. Carefully lift off cutout. Store, covered, at room temperature.   *Makes 16 cupcakes*

Hershey's Basic Cocoa Baking Mix: Stir together 4½ cups all-purpose flour, 2¾ cups sugar, 1¼ cups HERSHEY'S Cocoa, 1 tablespoon plus ½ teaspoon baking powder, 1¾ teaspoons salt and 1¼ teaspoons baking soda. Store in airtight container in cool, dry place for up to 1 month. Stir before using. Makes 8 cups mix.

Orange Glazed Pound Cake

Cinnamon Chip Applesauce Coffeecake

1 cup (2 sticks) butter or margarine, softened
1 cup granulated sugar
2 eggs
½ teaspoon vanilla extract
¾ cup applesauce
2½ cups all-purpose flour
1 teaspoon baking soda
½ teaspoon salt
1⅔ cups (10-ounce package) HERSHEY'S Cinnamon Chips
1 cup chopped pecans (optional)
¾ cup powdered sugar
1 to 2 tablespoons warm water

1. Heat oven to 350°F. Lightly grease 13×9×2-inch baking pan.

2. Beat butter and sugar with electric mixer on medium speed in large bowl until well blended. Beat in eggs and vanilla. Mix in applesauce. Stir together flour, baking soda and salt; gradually add to butter mixture, beating until well blended. Stir in cinnamon chips and pecans, if desired. Spread in prepared pan.

3. Bake 30 to 35 minutes or until wooden pick inserted in center comes out clean. Cool in pan on wire rack. Sprinkle cake with powdered sugar or stir together ¾ cup powdered sugar and warm water to make smooth glaze; drizzle over cake. Serve at room temperature or while still slightly warm. *Makes 12 to 15 servings*

Fluted Cake: Grease and flour 12-cup fluted tube pan. Prepare batter as directed; pour into prepared pan. Bake 45 to 50 minutes or until wooden pick inserted in thickest part comes out clean. Cool 15 minutes; invert onto wire rack. Cool completely.

Cupcakes: Line 24 baking cups (2½ inches in diameter) with paper baking liners. Prepare batter as directed; divide evenly into prepared cups. Bake 15 to 18 minutes or until wooden pick inserted in center comes out clean. Cool completely.

Cinnamon Chip Applesauce Coffeecake

Nestlé® Toll House® Chocolate Chip Pie

    2 large eggs
    ½ cup all-purpose flour
    ½ cup granulated sugar
    ½ cup packed brown sugar
    ¾ cup (1½ sticks) butter, softened
    1 cup (6 ounces) NESTLÉ® TOLL HOUSE® Semi-Sweet Chocolate Morsels
    1 cup chopped nuts
    1 *unbaked* 9-inch (4-cup volume) deep-dish pie shell*
      Sweetened whipped cream or ice cream (optional)

If using frozen pie shell, use deep-dish style, thawed completely. Bake on baking sheet; increase baking time slightly.

PREHEAT oven to 325°F.

BEAT eggs in large mixer bowl on high speed until foamy. Beat in flour, granulated sugar and brown sugar. Beat in butter. Stir in morsels and nuts. Spoon into pie shell.

BAKE for 55 to 60 minutes or until knife inserted halfway between outside edge and center comes out clean. Cool on wire rack. Serve warm with whipped cream. *Makes 8 servings*

Cherry Cupcakes

    1 (18¼-ounce) box chocolate cake mix
    3 eggs
    1⅓ cups water
    ½ cup vegetable oil
    1 (21-ounce) can cherry pie filling
    1 (16-ounce) can vanilla frosting

Prepare cake mix according to package directions, using eggs, water and oil. Spoon batter into 24 paper-lined muffin-pan cups, filling two-thirds full.

Remove 24 cherries from cherry filling; set aside. Spoon generous teaspoon of remaining cherry filling onto center of each cupcake.

Bake in preheated 350°F oven 20 to 25 minutes. Cool in pans on wire racks 10 minutes. Remove from pans. Let cool completely. Frost cupcakes with vanilla frosting. Garnish cupcakes with reserved cherries. *Makes 24 cupcakes*

*Favorite recipe from **Cherry Marketing Institute***

Pineapple Upside-Down Cake

        1 (8-ounce) can crushed pineapple in juice, undrained
        2 tablespoons margarine, melted, divided
        ½ cup firmly packed light brown sugar
        6 whole maraschino cherries
    1½ cups all-purpose flour
        2 tablespoons baking powder
        ¼ teaspoon salt
        1 cup granulated sugar
        ½ cup MOTT'S® Natural Apple Sauce
        1 whole egg
        3 egg whites, beaten until stiff

1. Preheat oven to 375°F. Drain pineapple; reserve juice. Spray sides of 8-inch square baking pan with nonstick cooking spray.

2. Spread 1 tablespoon melted margarine evenly in bottom of prepared pan. Sprinkle with brown sugar; top with pineapple. Slice cherries in half. Arrange cherries, cut side up, so that when cake is cut, each piece will have cherry half in center.

3. In small bowl, combine flour, baking powder and salt.

4. In large bowl, combine granulated sugar, apple sauce, whole egg, remaining 1 tablespoon melted margarine and reserved pineapple juice.

5. Add flour mixture to apple sauce mixture; stir until well blended. Fold in egg whites. Gently pour batter over fruit, spreading evenly.

6. Bake 35 to 40 minutes or until lightly browned. Cool on wire rack 10 minutes. Invert cake onto serving plate. Serve warm or cool completely. Cut into 12 pieces.   *Makes 12 servings*

Pineapple Upside-Down Cake

Citrus Pecan Pie

Crust

　　1 cup graham cracker crumbs (12 squares)
　　⅓ cup melted butter or margarine
　　¼ cup sugar
　　½ cup finely chopped pecans

Filling

　　½ cup sugar
　　½ cup cornstarch
　　1 cup freshly squeezed Texas Red Grapefruit juice with pulp (2 to 3 grapefruit)
　　1 cup freshly squeezed Texas Orange juice with pulp (4 to 5 oranges)
　　2 egg yolks, slightly beaten
　　1 tablespoon butter or margarine

Topping

　　Thawed whipped topping
　　6 to 8 pecan halves
　　Thin slices of grapefruit peel (optional)

Crust

Mix all ingredients together and press into bottom and up side of 9-inch pie pan. Chill crust 5 to 10 minutes before filling.

Filling

In medium saucepan, combine sugar and cornstarch. Stir in Texas Red Grapefruit juice and Texas Orange juice with pulp. Stir in egg yolks. Bring to a boil over medium heat, stirring constantly. Boil 1 minute. Remove from heat and stir in butter or margarine. Pour into pie crust. Refrigerate.

Topping

When ready to serve, add dollops of whipped topping around edge of pie and half of a pecan on top of topping for each piece of pie cut. For additional decoration, if desired, cut thin slices of peel from fruit. Using a small cookie cutter, cut out designs and place individually on top of the pie.

Makes 6 servings

Favorite recipe from **TexaSweet Citrus Marketing, Inc.**

Fudgy Ripple Cake

1 package (18.25 ounces) yellow cake mix, plus ingredients to prepare mix
1 package (3 ounces) cream cheese, softened
2 tablespoons unsweetened cocoa powder
  Fudgy Glaze (recipe follows)
½ cup "M&M's"® Chocolate Mini Baking Bits

Preheat oven to 350°F. Lightly grease and flour 10-inch Bundt or ring pan; set aside. Prepare cake mix as package directs. In medium bowl combine 1½ cups prepared batter, cream cheese and cocoa powder until smooth. Pour half of yellow batter into prepared pan. Drop spoonfuls of chocolate batter over yellow batter in pan. Top with remaining yellow batter. Bake about 45 minutes or until toothpick inserted near center comes out clean. Cool completely on wire rack. Unmold cake onto serving plate. Prepare Fudgy Glaze; spread over top of cake, allowing some glaze to run over side. Sprinkle with "M&M's"® Chocolate Mini Baking Bits. Store in tightly covered container.

Makes 10 servings

Fudgy Glaze

1 square (1 ounce) semi-sweet chocolate
1 cup powdered sugar
⅓ cup unsweetened cocoa powder
3 tablespoons milk
½ teaspoon vanilla extract

Place chocolate in small microwave-safe bowl. Microwave at HIGH 30 seconds; stir. Repeat as necessary until chocolate is completely melted, stirring at 10-second intervals; set aside. In medium bowl combine powdered sugar and cocoa powder. Stir in milk, vanilla and melted chocolate until smooth.

Classic Chocolate Cream Pie

2½ bars (1 ounce each) HERSHEY'S Unsweetened Baking Chocolate, broken into pieces
3 cups milk, divided
1⅓ cups sugar
3 tablespoons all-purpose flour
3 tablespoons cornstarch
½ teaspoon salt
3 egg yolks
2 tablespoons butter or margarine
1½ teaspoons vanilla extract
1 baked (9-inch) pie crust, cooled, or 1 (9-inch) crumb crust
Sweetened whipped cream (optional)

1. Combine chocolate and 2 cups milk in medium saucepan; cook over medium heat, stirring constantly, just until mixture boils. Remove from heat and set aside.

2. Stir together sugar, flour, cornstarch and salt in medium bowl. Whisk remaining 1 cup milk into egg yolks in separate bowl; stir into sugar mixture. Gradually add to chocolate mixture. Cook over medium heat, whisking constantly, until mixture boils; boil and stir 1 minute. Remove from heat; stir in butter and vanilla.

3. Pour into prepared crust; press plastic wrap directly onto surface. Cool; refrigerate until well chilled. Top with whipped cream, if desired.   *Makes 8 to 10 servings*

Dump Cake

1 can (20 ounces) crushed pineapple with juice, undrained
1 can (21 ounces) cherry pie filling
1 package DUNCAN HINES® Moist Deluxe® Classic Yellow Cake Mix
1 cup chopped pecans or walnuts
½ cup (1 stick) butter or margarine, cut into thin slices

1. Preheat oven to 350°F. Grease 13×9-inch pan.

2. Dump pineapple with juice into prepared pan. Spread evenly. Dump in pie filling. Spread evenly. Sprinkle cake mix evenly over cherry layer. Sprinkle pecans over cake mix. Dot with butter. Bake at 350°F for 50 minutes or until top is lightly browned. Serve warm or at room temperature.   *Makes 12 to 16 servings*

Tip: You can use DUNCAN HINES® Moist Deluxe® Pineapple Supreme Cake Mix in place of Moist Deluxe® Yellow Cake Mix.

Classic Chocolate Cream Pie

Angel Almond Cupcakes

   1 package DUNCAN HINES® Angel Food Cake Mix
1¼ cups water
   2 teaspoons almond extract
   1 container DUNCAN HINES® Wild Cherry Vanilla Frosting

1. Preheat oven to 350°F.

2. Combine cake mix, water and almond extract in large bowl. Beat at low speed with electric mixer until moistened. Beat at medium speed for 1 minute. Line medium muffin pans with paper baking cups. Fill muffin cups two-thirds full. Bake at 350°F for 20 to 25 minutes or until golden brown, cracked and dry on top. Remove from muffin pans. Cool completely. Frost with frosting. *Makes 30 to 32 cupcakes*

Cranberry Crumb Pie

   1 (9-inch) unbaked pie crust
   1 (8-ounce) package cream cheese, softened
   1 (14-ounce) can EAGLE BRAND® Sweetened Condensed Milk (NOT evaporated milk)
¼ cup lemon juice
   3 tablespoons light brown sugar, divided
   2 tablespoons cornstarch
   1 (16-ounce) can whole berry cranberry sauce
⅓ cup all-purpose flour
¼ cup (½ stick) cold butter or margarine
¾ cup chopped walnuts

1. Preheat oven to 425°F. Bake pie crust 6 minutes; remove from oven. Reduce oven temperature to 375°F.

2. In large bowl, beat cream cheese until fluffy. Gradually beat in EAGLE BRAND® until smooth. Stir in lemon juice. Pour into baked crust.

3. In small bowl, combine 1 tablespoon brown sugar and cornstarch; mix well. Stir in cranberry sauce. Spoon evenly over cheese mixture.

4. In medium bowl, cut butter into flour and remaining 2 tablespoons brown sugar until crumbly. Stir in walnuts. Sprinkle evenly over cranberry mixture. Bake 45 to 50 minutes or until bubbly and golden. Cool. Serve at room temperature or chill thoroughly. Store leftovers covered in refrigerator. *Makes one (9-inch) pie*

Angel Almond Cupcakes

Double Chocolate Snack Cake

1 package DUNCAN HINES® Moist Deluxe® Devil's Food Cake Mix, plus ingredients to prepare mix
1 cup white chocolate chips, divided
½ cup semisweet chocolate chips

1. Preheat oven to 350°F. Grease and flour 13×9-inch pan.

2. Prepare cake mix as directed on package. Stir in ½ cup white chocolate chips and semisweet chocolate chips. Pour into prepared pan. Bake at 350°F for 35 to 40 minutes or until toothpick inserted in center comes out clean. Remove from oven; sprinkle top with remaining ½ cup white chocolate chips. Serve warm or cool completely in pan.   *Makes 12 to 16 servings*

Tip: For a special dessert, serve cake warm with a scoop of vanilla ice cream or whipped cream garnished with the chocolate chips.

Orange Pecan Pie

3 eggs
½ cup GRANDMA'S® Molasses
½ cup light corn syrup
¼ cup orange juice
1 teaspoon grated orange peel
1 teaspoon vanilla
1½ cups whole pecan halves
1 (9-inch) unbaked pie shell
   Whipped cream (optional)

Heat oven to 350°F. In large bowl, beat eggs. Add molasses, corn syrup, orange juice, orange peel and vanilla; beat until well blended. Stir in pecans. Pour into unbaked pie shell. Bake 30 to 45 minutes or until filling sets. Cool on wire rack. Garnish as desired. Serve with whipped cream, if desired.   *Makes 8 servings*

Double Chocolate Snack Cake

Pineapple Fruit Tart

¼ cup ground almonds (about 2 tablespoons whole almonds)
¼ cup butter or margarine, softened
¼ cup sugar
2 tablespoons milk
½ teaspoon almond extract
¾ cup all-purpose flour
2 packages (3 ounces each) cream cheese, softened
2 tablespoons sour cream
¼ cup apricot preserves, divided
1 teaspoon vanilla extract
1 can (15¼ ounces) DEL MONTE® Sliced Pineapple In Its Own Juice, drained and cut in halves
2 kiwifruits, peeled, sliced and cut into halves
1 cup sliced strawberries

1. Combine almonds, butter, sugar, milk and almond extract; mix well. Blend in flour. Chill dough 1 hour.

2. Press dough evenly onto bottom and up side of tart pan with removable bottom.

3. Bake at 350°F. 15 to 18 minutes or until golden brown. Cool.

4. Combine cream cheese, sour cream, 1 tablespoon apricot preserves and vanilla. Spread onto crust. Arrange pineapple, kiwi and strawberries over cream cheese mixture.

5. Heat remaining 3 tablespoons apricot preserves in small saucepan over low heat. Spoon over fruit.

Makes 8 servings

Cookies & Treats

Cookies are easy to make, quick to bake and, most of all, fun to eat. Fill the cookie jar with Jumbo 3-Chip Cookies or Coconut Macaroons and don't be surprised when it empties out in a flash. Wow the after-school crowd with Hershey's Best Brownies or S'Morffins. You'll find treats in all your family's favorite flavors—banana, peppermint, coconut, lemon, butterscotch, peanut butter and plenty of chocolate, of course! There are so many delicious options, picking which one to try first will be a sweet dilemma.

Fluted Kisses® Cups with
Peanut Butter Filling (page 356)

Cut-Out Cookies

3½ cups all-purpose flour
2 teaspoons baking powder
¼ teaspoon salt
1 (14-ounce) can EAGLE BRAND® Sweetened Condensed Milk (NOT evaporated milk)
¾ cup (1½ sticks) butter or margarine, softened
2 eggs
1 tablespoon vanilla extract
Colored sugar sprinkles (optional)
Powdered Sugar Glaze (recipe follows, optional)

1. Combine flour, baking powder and salt. In large bowl with mixer on low speed, beat EAGLE BRAND®, butter, eggs and vanilla until just blended. Beat on medium speed 1 minute or until smooth. Add flour mixture; beat on low speed until blended. (If using hand-held mixer, use wooden spoon to add last portion of flour mixture.) Divide dough into thirds. Wrap and chill dough 2 hours or until easy to handle.

2. Preheat oven to 350°F. On lightly floured surface, roll out one portion of dough to ⅛-inch thickness. Cut out shapes. Gather dough and re-roll to use entire portion of dough. Repeat with remaining dough portions. Place cut-outs 1 inch apart on ungreased baking sheets. Sprinkle with colored sugar (optional). Bake 9 to 11 minutes, or until lightly browned around edges (do not overbake). Cool 5 minutes. Remove cookies to wire racks. When cool, glaze and decorate as desired. Store covered at room temperature. *Makes 5½ dozen cookies*

Tip: Freeze Cut-Out Cookies in a tightly sealed container.

Powdered Sugar Glaze

2 cups sifted confectioners' sugar
½ teaspoon vanilla extract
2 tablespoons milk or whipping cream
Food coloring (optional)

Whisk powdered sugar and vanilla, adding just enough milk or cream to bind into a glaze consistency. Add food coloring (optional) to tint glaze.

Cut-Out Cookies

Watermelon Banana Split

2 bananas
1 medium watermelon
1 cup fresh blueberries
1 cup diced fresh pineapple
1 cup sliced fresh strawberries
¼ cup caramel fruit dip
¼ cup honey roasted almonds

Peel bananas and cut in half lengthwise then cut each piece in half. For each serving, lay 2 banana pieces against sides of shallow dish. Using an ice cream scooper, place three watermelon "scoops" in between each banana in each dish. Remove seeds if necessary. Top each watermelon "scoop" with a different fresh fruit topping. Drizzle caramel fruit dip over all. Sprinkle with almonds.

Makes 4 servings

*Favorite recipe from **National Watermelon Promotion Board***

S'Morffins

6 BAYS® English Muffins, lightly toasted and buttered
8 milk chocolate bars (1.55 ounces each) divided
3 cups miniature marshmallows, divided
3 pints super-premium vanilla ice cream
1½ cups coarsely chopped and toasted walnuts, divided
    Hot fudge or caramel sauce, warmed (optional)

Place muffins on foil-lined baking sheet. Break chocolate bars into squares. Top each muffin half with eight chocolate squares. Broil, in preheated broiler, to just lightly melt chocolate. Arrange ¼ cup marshmallows on each muffin half; press into melted chocolate. Broil muffins about 6 inches from heat source, until the marshmallows are puffed and golden brown and chocolate has melted. Scoop ice cream onto prepared muffin halves; then top with 2 tablespoons walnuts. Spoon heated fudge or caramel sauce over each S'Morffin, if desired. Serve immediately.

Makes 12 servings

Tip: Rotate pan to toast marshmallows evenly.

Watermelon Banana Split

Milk Chocolate Florentine Cookies

⅔ cup butter
2 cups quick oats
1 cup granulated sugar
⅔ cup all-purpose flour
¼ cup light or dark corn syrup
¼ cup milk
1 teaspoon vanilla extract
¼ teaspoon salt
1¾ cups (11.5-ounce package) NESTLÉ® TOLL HOUSE® Milk Chocolate Morsels

PREHEAT oven to 375°F. Line baking sheets with foil.

MELT butter in medium saucepan; remove from heat. Stir in oats, sugar, flour, corn syrup, milk, vanilla extract and salt; mix well. Drop by level teaspoon, about 3 inches apart, onto prepared baking sheets. Spread thinly with rubber spatula.

BAKE for 6 to 8 minutes or until golden brown. Cool completely on baking sheets on wire racks. Peel foil from cookies.

MICROWAVE morsels in medium, uncovered, microwave-safe bowl on MEDIUM-HIGH (70%) power for 1 minute. Stir. Morsels may retain some of their original shape. If necessary, microwave at additional 10- to 15-second intervals, stirring just until morsels are melted. Spread thin layer of melted chocolate onto flat side of *half* the cookies. Top with *remaining* cookies.

Makes about 3½ dozen sandwich cookies

Chocolate Truffle Cups

1 (7-ounce) package ALOUETTE® Cuisine™ Crème Fraîche
8 ounces good quality white or bittersweet chocolate broken into small pieces
1 tablespoon liqueur, such as almond, coffee or orange (optional)
1 (2-ounce) package frozen mini phyllo shells

Heat crème fraîche over medium heat until it softens to a thick liquid consistency. Remove from heat and add chocolate. Stir until chocolate is melted and mixture is smooth. Add liqueur, if desired. Refrigerate for 1 hour or until set. Pipe into phyllo shells and serve.

Makes 15 dessert cups

Milk Chocolate Florentine Cookies

Gingersnaps

2½ cups all-purpose flour
1½ teaspoons ground ginger
1 teaspoon baking soda
1 teaspoon ground allspice
½ teaspoon salt
1½ cups sugar
2 tablespoons margarine, softened
½ cup MOTT'S® Apple Sauce
¼ cup GRANDMA'S® Molasses

1. Preheat oven to 375°F. Spray cookie sheets with nonstick cooking spray.

2. In medium bowl, sift together flour, ginger, baking soda, allspice and salt.

3. In large bowl, beat sugar and margarine with electric mixer at medium speed until blended. Whisk in apple sauce and molasses.

4. Add flour mixture to apple sauce mixture; stir until well blended.

5. Drop rounded tablespoonfuls of dough 1 inch apart onto prepared cookie sheets. Flatten each slightly with moistened fingertips.

6. Bake 12 to 15 minutes or until firm. Cool completely on wire rack. *Makes 3 dozen cookies*

Banana Smoothies & Pops

1 (14-ounce) can EAGLE BRAND® Sweetened Condensed Milk (NOT evaporated milk)
1 (8-ounce) container vanilla yogurt
2 ripe bananas
½ cup orange juice

1. In blender container, combine all ingredients; blend until smooth, scraping down sides occasionally.

2. Serve immediately. Store leftovers covered in refrigerator. *Makes 4 cups*

Banana Smoothie Pops: Spoon banana mixture into 8 (5-ounce) paper cups. Freeze 30 minutes. Insert wooden craft sticks into center of each cup; freeze until firm. Makes 8 pops

Fruit Smoothies: Substitute 1 cup of your favorite fruit and ½ cup any fruit juice for banana and orange juice.

Prep Time: 5 minutes

Gingersnaps

Chocolate Almond Biscotti

1 package DUNCAN HINES® Moist Deluxe® Dark Chocolate Cake Mix
1 cup all-purpose flour
½ cup butter or margarine, melted
2 eggs
1 teaspoon almond extract
½ cup chopped almonds
    White chocolate, melted (optional)

1. Preheat oven to 350°F. Line 2 baking sheets with parchment paper.

2. Combine cake mix, flour, butter, eggs and almond extract in large bowl. Beat at low speed with electric mixer until well blended; stir in almonds. Divide dough in half. Shape each half into 12×2-inch log; place logs on prepared baking sheets. (Bake logs separately.)

3. Bake at 350°F for 30 to 35 minutes or until toothpick inserted in center comes out clean. Remove logs from oven; cool on baking sheets 15 minutes. Using serrated knife, cut logs into ½-inch slices. Arrange slices on baking sheets. Bake biscotti 10 minutes. Remove to cooling racks; cool completely.

4. Dip one end of each biscotti in melted white chocolate, if desired. Allow chocolate to set before storing biscotti in airtight container. *Makes about 2½ dozen cookies*

Jingle Jumbles

¾ cup butter or margarine, softened
1 cup packed brown sugar
¼ cup molasses
1 egg
2¼ cups unsifted all-purpose flour
2 teaspoons baking soda
1 teaspoon *each* ground ginger and ground cinnamon
½ teaspoon *each* salt and ground cloves
1¼ cups SUN•MAID® Raisins
    Granulated sugar

In large bowl, cream butter and sugar. Add molasses and egg; beat until fluffy. In medium bowl, sift together flour, baking soda, ginger, cinnamon, salt and cloves. Stir into molasses mixture. Stir in raisins. Cover and chill about 30 minutes.Preheat oven to 375°F. Grease cookie sheets. Form dough into 1½-inch balls; roll in granulated sugar, coating generously. Place 2 inches apart on prepared cookie sheets. Bake 12 to 14 minutes or until edges are firm and centers are still slightly soft. Remove to wire racks to cool. *Makes about 2 dozen cookies*

Chocolate Almond Biscotti

Rice Pudding

3 cups 2% low-fat milk
1 large stick cinnamon
1 cup uncooked rice*
2 cups water
½ teaspoon salt
  Peel of orange or lemon
¾ cup sugar
¼ cup raisins
2 tablespoons dark rum

Recipe based on regular-milled long grain white rice.

Heat milk and cinnamon in small saucepan over medium heat until milk is infused with flavor of cinnamon, about 15 minutes. Combine rice, water, and salt in 2- to 3-quart saucepan. Bring to a boil; stir once or twice. Place orange peel on top of rice. Reduce heat; cover and simmer 15 minutes or until rice is tender and liquid is absorbed. Remove and discard orange peel. Strain milk and stir into cooked rice. Add sugar and simmer 20 minutes or until thickened, stirring often. Add raisins and rum; simmer 10 minutes. Serve hot. To reheat, add a little milk to restore creamy texture.   *Makes 6 servings*

Tip: Use medium or short grain rice for rice pudding with a creamier consistency.

*Favorite recipe from **USA Rice***

Marvelous Macaroons

1 can (8 ounces) DOLE® Crushed Pineapple
1 can (14 ounces) sweetened condensed milk
1 package (7 ounces) flaked coconut
½ cup margarine, melted
½ cup chopped almonds, toasted
1 teaspoon grated lemon peel
¼ teaspoon almond extract
1 cup all-purpose flour
1 teaspoon baking powder

• Preheat oven to 350°F. Drain crushed pineapple well, pressing out excess juice with back of spoon. In large bowl, combine drained pineapple, milk, coconut, margarine, almonds, lemon peel and almond extract.

• In small bowl, combine flour and baking powder. Beat into pineapple mixture until blended. Drop heaping tablespoonfuls of dough 1 inch apart onto greased cookie sheets.

• Bake 13 to 15 minutes or until lightly browned. Garnish with whole almonds, if desired. Cool on wire racks. Store in covered container in refrigerator.   *Makes about 3½ dozen cookies*

Design Your Own Chocolate Cookie

1 cup (2 sticks) butter, softened
1 cup granulated sugar
¾ cup packed light brown sugar
2 teaspoons vanilla extract
½ teaspoon salt
2 eggs
2 cups all-purpose flour
½ cup HERSHEY'S Cocoa
1 teaspoon baking soda

1. Heat oven to 375°F.

2. Beat butter, granulated sugar, brown sugar, vanilla and salt in large bowl until creamy. Add eggs; beat well.

3. Stir together flour, cocoa and baking soda; gradually add to butter mixture, beating until well blended. Drop by rounded teaspoons onto ungreased cookie sheet.

4. Bake 8 to 10 minutes or until set. Cool slightly; remove from cookie sheet to wire rack. Cool completely. *Makes about 5 dozen cookies*

Chocolate Chocolate Chip Cookies: Add 2 cups (one 12- or 11.5-ounce package) HERSHEY'S Semi-Sweet MINI CHIPS™, SPECIAL DARK® or Milk Chocolate Chips to basic chocolate batter.

Mini Kisses® Chocolate Cookies: Add 1¾ cups (10-ounce package) HERSHEY'S MINI KISSES® Milk Chocolates to basic chocolate batter.

Mint Chocolate Chip Cookies: Add 1⅔ cups (10-ounce package) HERSHEY'S Mint Chocolate Chips to basic chocolate batter.

Chocolate Cookies with White Chips: Add 2 cups (12-ounce package) HERSHEY'S Premier White Chips to basic chocolate batter.

Chocolate Cookies with Peanut Butter Chips: Add 1⅔ cups (one 10- or 11-ounce package) REESE'S® Peanut Butter Chips or REESE'S® Peanut Butter and Milk Chocolate Chips to basic chocolate batter

Chocolate Cookies with Toffee: Add 1 to 1¼ cups HEATH® BITS 'O BRICKLE® Toffee Bits or HEATH® Milk Chocolate Toffee Bits to basic chocolate batter. Lightly grease or paper-line cookie sheets.

Reese's® Double Peanut Butter and Milk Chocolate Chip Cookies

½ cup (1 stick) butter or margarine, softened
¾ cup sugar
⅓ cup REESE'S® Creamy or Crunchy Peanut Butter
1 egg
½ teaspoon vanilla extract
1¼ cups all-purpose flour
½ teaspoon baking soda
¼ teaspoon salt
1¾ cups (11-ounce package) REESE'S® Peanut Butter and Milk Chocolate Chips

Heat oven to 350°F. Beat butter, sugar and peanut butter in medium bowl until creamy. Add egg and vanilla; beat well. Stir together flour, baking soda and salt; add to butter mixture, blending well. Stir in chips. Drop by rounded teaspoons onto ungreased cookie sheets. Bake 12 to 14 minutes or until light golden brown around the edges. Cool 1 minute on cookie sheets. Remove to wire rack; cool completely. *Makes about 3 dozen cookies*

Lemon Cake-Top Pudding

¼ cup sliced natural almonds
4 large eggs, separated
1 cup sugar
3 tablespoons margarine, softened
3 tablespoons all-purpose flour
⅛ teaspoon salt
⅓ cup freshly squeezed SUNKIST® lemon juice, plus grated peel of ½ SUNKIST® lemon
1 cup reduced-fat or lowfat milk

Preheat oven to 325°F. Spray 1½-quart glass casserole with butter-flavored nonstick cooking spray. Sprinkle almonds over bottom. In medium bowl, with electric mixer, beat egg whites at high speed until soft peaks form. Gradually add ¼ cup sugar, beating until medium-stiff peaks form; set aside. In large bowl, beat together margarine and remaining ¾ cup sugar. In small bowl, beat egg yolks well; add to margarine-sugar mixture, beating thoroughly. Add flour, salt and lemon juice; beat well. Stir in lemon peel and milk until blended. Stir in ⅓ of the egg white mixture, then gently fold in remaining egg whites. Pour batter into prepared casserole over almonds. Place casserole in shallow baking pan filled with 1 inch hot water. Bake, uncovered, for 50 to 55 minutes, or until golden brown and top springs back when lightly touched with finger. Carefully remove from water and let set for 20 to 30 minutes. Serve warm or chilled. *Makes 6 to 8 servings*

Reese's® Double Peanut Butter and Milk Chocolate Chip Cookies

Dipsy Doodles Butterscotch Dip

1 (14-ounce) can EAGLE BRAND® Sweetened Condensed Milk (NOT evaporated milk)
1½ cups milk
1 (4-serving-size) package cook-and-serve butterscotch pudding and pie filling mix
Apples or pears, cored and sliced, or banana chunks

1. In medium saucepan, over medium heat, combine EAGLE BRAND®, milk and pudding mix. Cook and stir until thickened and bubbly; cook 2 minutes more.

2. Cool slightly. Pour into serving bowl or individual cups. Serve warm with fruit.

Makes about 2½ cups dip

Tip: Store leftovers covered in the refrigerator. Reheat and serve as a sauce over vanilla ice cream. Sprinkle sauce with miniature semisweet chocolate chips or toasted nuts, if desired.

Prep Time: 15 minutes

Fluted Kisses® Cups
with Peanut Butter Filling

72 HERSHEY'S KISSES® Brand Milk Chocolates, divided
1 cup REESE'S® Creamy Peanut Butter
1 cup powdered sugar
1 tablespoon butter or margarine, softened

1. Line small baking cups (1¾ inches in diameter) with small paper bake cups. Remove wrappers from chocolates.

2. Place 48 chocolates in small microwave-safe bowl. Microwave on HIGH (100%) 1 minute or until chocolate is melted and smooth when stirred. Using small brush, coat inside of paper cups with melted chocolate.

3. Refrigerate 20 minutes; reapply melted chocolate to any thin spots. Refrigerate until firm, preferably overnight. Gently peel paper from chocolate cups.

4. Beat peanut butter, powdered sugar and butter with electric mixer on medium speed in small bowl until smooth. Spoon into chocolate cups. Before serving, top each cup with a chocolate piece. Cover; store cups in refrigerator.

Makes about 2 dozen pieces

Dipsy Doodles Butterscotch Dip

Pumpkin Spiced and Iced Cookies

2¼ cups all-purpose flour
1½ teaspoons pumpkin pie spice
1 teaspoon baking powder
½ teaspoon baking soda
½ teaspoon salt
1 cup (2 sticks) butter or margarine, softened
1 cup granulated sugar
1 can (15 ounces) LIBBY'S® 100% Pure Pumpkin
2 large eggs
1 teaspoon vanilla extract
2 cups (12-ounce package) NESTLÉ® TOLL HOUSE® Semi-Sweet Chocolate Morsels
1 cup chopped walnuts (optional)
Vanilla Glaze (recipe follows)

PREHEAT oven to 375°F. Grease baking sheets.

COMBINE flour, pumpkin pie spice, baking powder, baking soda and salt in medium bowl. Beat butter and granulated sugar in large mixer bowl until creamy. Beat in pumpkin, eggs and vanilla extract. Gradually beat in flour mixture. Stir in morsels and nuts. Drop by rounded tablespoon onto prepared baking sheets.

BAKE for 15 to 20 minutes or until edges are lightly browned. Cool on baking sheets for 2 minutes; remove to wire racks to cool completely. Spread or drizzle with Vanilla Glaze.

Makes about 5½ dozen cookies

Vanilla Glaze: **COMBINE** 1 cup powdered sugar, 1 to 1½ tablespoons milk and ½ teaspoon vanilla extract in small bowl; mix well.

Pumpkin Spiced and Iced Cookies

Peanut Butter Fudge Brownie Bars

1 cup (2 sticks) butter or margarine, melted
1½ cups sugar
2 eggs
1 teaspoon vanilla extract
1¼ cups all-purpose flour
⅔ cup HERSHEY'S Cocoa
¼ cup milk
1¼ cups chopped pecans or walnuts, divided
½ cup (1 stick) butter or margarine
1⅔ cups (10-ounce package) REESE'S® Peanut Butter Chips
1 can (14 ounces) sweetened condensed milk (not evaporated milk)
¼ cup HERSHEY'S Semi-Sweet Chocolate Chips

1. Heat oven to 350°F. Grease 13×9×2-inch baking pan.

2. Beat melted butter, sugar, eggs and vanilla in large bowl with electric mixer on medium speed until well blended. Add flour, cocoa and milk; beat until blended. Stir in 1 cup nuts. Spread in prepared pan.

3. Bake 25 to 30 minutes or just until edges begin to pull away from sides of pan. Cool completely in pan on wire rack.

4. Melt ½ cup butter and peanut butter chips in medium saucepan over low heat, stirring constantly. Add sweetened condensed milk, stirring until smooth; pour over baked layer.

5. Place chocolate chips in small microwave-safe bowl. Microwave at HIGH (100%) 45 seconds or just until chips are melted when stirred. Drizzle bars with melted chocolate; sprinkle with remaining ¼ cup nuts. Refrigerate 1 hour or until firm. Cut into bars. Cover; refrigerate leftovers.

Makes 36 bars

Peanut Butter Fudge Brownie Bars

Coconut Macaroons

1 (14-ounce) can EAGLE BRAND® Sweetened Condensed Milk (NOT evaporated milk)
1 egg white, whipped
2 teaspoons vanilla extract
1½ teaspoons almond extract
1 (14-ounce) package flaked coconut

1. Preheat oven to 325°F. Line baking sheets with foil; grease and flour foil. Set aside.

2. In large bowl, combine EAGLE BRAND®, egg white, extracts and coconut; mix well. Drop by rounded teaspoonfuls onto prepared baking sheets; slightly flatten each mound with a spoon.

3. Bake 15 to 17 minutes or until lightly browned around edges. Immediately remove from baking sheets (macaroons will stick if allowed to cool); cool on wire racks. Store loosely covered at room temperature. *Makes about 4 dozen cookies*

Prep Time: 10 minutes
Bake Time: 15 to 17 minutes

Hershey's Best Brownies

1 cup (2 sticks) butter or margarine
2 cups sugar
2 teaspoons vanilla extract
4 eggs
¾ cup HERSHEY'S Cocoa or HERSHEY'S SPECIAL DARK® Cocoa
1 cup all-purpose flour
½ teaspoon baking powder
¼ teaspoon salt
1 cup chopped nuts (optional)

1. Heat oven to 350°F. Grease 13×9×2-inch baking pan.

2. Place butter in large microwave-safe bowl. Microwave at HIGH (100%) 2 to 2½ minutes or until melted. Stir in sugar and vanilla. Add eggs, one at a time, beating well with spoon after each addition. Add cocoa; beat until well blended. Add flour, baking powder and salt; beat well. Stir in nuts, if desired. Pour batter into prepared pan.

3. Bake 30 to 35 minutes or until brownies begin to pull away from sides of pan. Cool completely in pan on wire rack. Cut into bars. *Makes about 36 brownies*

Coconut Macaroons

Baked Apple Crisp

8 cups thinly sliced unpeeled apples (about 8 medium)
2 tablespoons granulated sugar
4½ teaspoons lemon juice
4 teaspoons ground cinnamon, divided
1½ cups MOTT'S® Natural Apple Sauce
1 cup uncooked rolled oats
½ cup firmly packed light brown sugar
⅓ cup all-purpose flour
⅓ cup evaporated skimmed milk
¼ cup nonfat dry milk powder
1 cup vanilla nonfat yogurt

1. Preheat oven to 350°F. Spray 2-quart casserole dish with nonstick cooking spray.

2. In large bowl, toss apple slices with granulated sugar, lemon juice and 2 teaspoons cinnamon. Spoon into prepared dish. Spread apple sauce evenly over apple mixture.

3. In medium bowl, combine oats, brown sugar, flour, evaporated milk, dry milk powder and remaining 2 teaspoons cinnamon. Spread over apple sauce.

4. Bake 35 to 40 minutes or until lightly browned and bubbly. Cool slightly; serve warm. Top each serving with dollop of yogurt.

Makes 12 servings

"M&M's"® Jam Sandwiches

½ cup (1 stick) butter, softened
¾ cup granulated sugar
1 large egg
1 teaspoon almond extract
½ teaspoon vanilla extract
1⅓ cups all-purpose flour
¼ teaspoon baking powder
¼ teaspoon salt
   Powdered sugar
½ cup seedless raspberry jam
½ cup "M&M's"® Chocolate Mini Baking Bits

In large bowl cream butter and sugar until light and fluffy; beat in egg, almond extract and vanilla. In small bowl combine flour, baking powder and salt; blend into creamed mixture. Wrap and refrigerate dough 2 to 3 hours. Preheat oven to 375°F. Working with half the dough at a time on lightly floured surface, roll to ⅛-inch thickness. Cut into desired shapes using 3-inch cookie cutters. Cut out equal numbers of each shape. (If dough becomes too soft, refrigerate several minutes before continuing.) Cut 1½- to 2-inch centers out of half the cookies of each shape. Reroll trimmings and cut out more cookies. Using rigid spatula, carefully transfer shapes to ungreased cookie sheets. Bake 7 to 9 minutes. Cool on cookie sheets 1 to 2 minutes; cool completely on wire racks. Sprinkle powdered sugar on cookies with holes. Spread about 1 teaspoon jam on flat side of whole cookies, spreading almost to edges. Place cookies with holes, flat side down, over jam. Place "M&M's"® Chocolate Mini Baking Bits over jam in holes. Store between layers of waxed paper in tightly covered container.

Makes 1 dozen sandwich cookies

Jumbo 3-Chip Cookies

4 cups all-purpose flour
1 teaspoon baking powder
1 teaspoon baking soda
1½ cups (3 sticks) butter, softened
1¼ cups granulated sugar
1¼ cups packed brown sugar
2 large eggs
1 tablespoon vanilla extract
1 cup (6 ounces) NESTLÉ® TOLL HOUSE® Milk Chocolate Morsels
1 cup (6 ounces) NESTLÉ® TOLL HOUSE® Semi-Sweet Chocolate Morsels
½ cup NESTLÉ® TOLL HOUSE® Premier White Morsels
1 cup chopped nuts

PREHEAT oven to 375°F.

COMBINE flour, baking powder and baking soda in medium bowl. Beat butter, granulated sugar and brown sugar in large mixer bowl until creamy. Beat in eggs and vanilla extract. Gradually beat in flour mixture. Stir in morsels and nuts. Drop dough by level ¼-cup measure 2 inches apart onto ungreased baking sheets.

BAKE for 12 to 14 minutes or until light golden brown. Cool on baking sheets for 2 minutes; remove to wire racks to cool completely. *Makes about 2 dozen cookies*

Crunchy Peppermint Candy Ice Cream

1¼ cups water
1 (14-ounce) can EAGLE BRAND® Sweetened Condensed Milk (NOT evaporated milk)
2 cups (1 pint) light cream
½ cup crushed hard peppermint candy
1 tablespoon vanilla extract

1. Combine all ingredients in ice cream freezer container. Freeze according to manufacturer's instructions.

2. Garnish with additional crushed peppermint candy (optional). Freeze leftovers.
Makes 1½ quarts

Jumbo 3-Chip Cookies

Banana Split Cups

1 package (18 ounces) refrigerated chocolate chip cookie dough
⅔ cup "M&M's"® Chocolate Mini Baking Bits, divided
1 ripe medium banana, cut into 18 slices and halved
¾ cup chocolate syrup, divided
2¼ cups any flavor ice cream, softened
   Aerosol whipped topping
¼ cup chopped maraschino cherries

Lightly grease 36 (1¾-inch) mini muffin cups. Cut dough into 36 equal pieces; roll into balls. Place 1 ball in bottom of each muffin cup. Press dough onto bottoms and up sides of muffin cups; chill 15 minutes. Press ⅓ cup "M&M's"® Chocolate Mini Baking Bits into bottoms and sides of dough cups. Preheat oven to 350°F. Bake cookies 8 to 9 minutes. Cookies will be puffy. Remove from oven; gently press down center of each cookie. Return to oven 1 minute. Cool cookies in muffin cups 5 minutes. Remove to wire racks; cool completely. Place 1 banana half slice in each cookie cup; top with ½ teaspoon chocolate syrup. Place about ½ teaspoon "M&M's"® Chocolate Mini Baking Bits in each cookie cup; top with 1 tablespoon ice cream. Top each cookie cup with ½ teaspoon chocolate syrup, whipped topping, remaining "M&M's"® Chocolate Mini Baking Bits and 1 maraschino cherry piece. Store covered in freezer. *Makes 3 dozen cookies*

Crispy's Irresistible Peanut Butter Marbles

1 package (18 ounces) refrigerated peanut butter cookie dough
2 cups "M&M's"® Milk Chocolate Mini Baking Bits, divided
1 cup crisp rice cereal, divided (optional)
1 package (18 ounces) refrigerated sugar cookie dough
¼ cup unsweetened cocoa powder

In large bowl combine peanut butter dough, 1 cup "M&M's"® Milk Chocolate Mini Baking Bits and ½ cup cereal, if desired. Remove dough to small bowl; set aside. In large bowl combine sugar dough and cocoa powder until well blended. Stir in remaining 1 cup "M&M's"® Milk Chocolate Mini Baking Bits and remaining ½ cup cereal, if desired. Remove half the dough to small bowl; set aside. Combine half the peanut butter dough with half the chocolate dough by folding together just enough to marble. Shape marbled dough into 8×2-inch log. Wrap log in plastic wrap. Repeat with remaining doughs. Refrigerate logs 2 hours. To bake, preheat oven to 350°F. Cut dough into ¼-inch-thick slices. Place about 2 inches apart on ungreased cookie sheets. Bake 12 to 14 minutes. Cool 1 minute on cookie sheets; cool completely on wire racks. Store in tightly covered container. *Makes 5 dozen cookies*

Banana Split Cups

Coconutty "M&M's"® Brownies

6 squares (1 ounce each) semi-sweet chocolate
¾ cup granulated sugar
½ cup (1 stick) butter
2 large eggs
1 tablespoon vegetable oil
1 teaspoon vanilla extract
1¼ cups all-purpose flour
3 tablespoons unsweetened cocoa powder
1 teaspoon baking powder
½ teaspoon salt
1½ cups "M&M's"® Chocolate Mini Baking Bits, divided
Coconut Topping (recipe follows)

Preheat oven to 350°F. Lightly grease 8×8×2-inch baking pan; set aside. In small saucepan combine chocolate, sugar and butter over low heat; stir constantly until chocolate is melted. Remove from heat; let cool slightly. In large bowl beat eggs, oil and vanilla; stir in chocolate mixture until well blended. In medium bowl combine flour, cocoa powder, baking powder and salt; add to chocolate mixture. Stir in 1 cup "M&M's"® Chocolate Mini Baking Bits. Spread batter evenly in prepared pan. Bake 35 to 40 minutes or until toothpick inserted in center comes out clean. Cool completely on wire rack. Prepare Coconut Topping. Spread over brownies; sprinkle with remaining ½ cup "M&M's"® Chocolate Mini Baking Bits. Cut into bars. Store in tightly covered container.   *Makes 16 brownies*

Coconut Topping

½ cup (1 stick) butter
⅓ cup firmly packed light brown sugar
⅓ cup light corn syrup
1 cup sweetened shredded coconut, toasted*
¾ cup chopped pecans
1 teaspoon vanilla extract

*To toast coconut, spread evenly on cookie sheet. Toast in preheated 350°F oven 7 to 8 minutes or until golden brown, stirring occasionally.

In large saucepan melt butter over medium heat; add brown sugar and corn syrup, stirring constantly until thick and bubbly. Remove from heat and stir in remaining ingredients.

Acknowledgments

The publisher would like to thank the companies and organizations listed below for the use of their recipes and photographs in this publication.

ACH Food Companies, Inc.

American Lamb Council

Australian Lamb

Bays English Muffin Corporation

Alouette® Cheese, Chavrie® Cheese, Saladena®

Birds Eye Foods

Bob Evans®

Cabot® Creamery Cooperative

California Wild Rice Advisory Board

Cherry Marketing Institute

Clamato® is a registered trademark of Mott's, LLP

Crisco is a registered trademark of The J.M. Smucker Company

Del Monte Corporation

Dole Food Company, Inc.

Duncan Hines® and Moist Deluxe® are registered trademarks of Pinnacle Foods Corp.

EAGLE BRAND®

Equal® sweetener

Filippo Berio® Olive Oil

Florida Department of Agriculture and Consumer Services, Bureau of Seafood and Aquaculture

The Golden Grain Company®

Grandma's® is a registered trademark of Mott's, LLP

The Hershey Company

The Hidden Valley® Food Products Company

Hillshire Farm®

Holland House® is a registered trademark of Mott's, LLP

Hormel Foods, LLC

Jennie-O Turkey Store®

Jif® trademark of The J.M. Smucker Company

JOLLY TIME® Pop Corn

Kahlúa® Liqueur

The Kingsford® Products Co.

© Mars, Incorporated 2006

MASTERFOODS USA

McIlhenny Company (TABASCO® brand Pepper Sauce)

Minnesota Cultivated Wild Rice Council

Mott's® is a registered trademark of Mott's, LLP

Mushroom Information Center

National Chicken Council / US Poultry & Egg Association

National Honey Board

National Onion Association

National Pork Board

National Watermelon Promotion Board

NatraTaste® is a registered trademark of Stadt Holding Corporation

Nestlé USA

Ortega®, A Division of B&G Foods, Inc.

Reckitt Benckiser Inc.

RED STAR® Yeast, a product of Lasaffre Yeast Corporation

Riviana Foods Inc.

StarKist Seafood Company

Sun•Maid® Growers of California

Reprinted with permission of Sunkist Growers, Inc. All Rights Reserved.

TexaSweet Citrus Marketing, Inc.

Unilever

USA Rice Federation

Veg•All®

Walnut Marketing Board

Washington Apple Commission

Watkins Incorporated

Wisconsin Milk Marketing Board

Index

Metric Conversion Chart

VOLUME MEASUREMENTS (dry)

$1/8$ teaspoon = 0.5 mL
$1/4$ teaspoon = 1 mL
$1/2$ teaspoon = 2 mL
$3/4$ teaspoon = 4 mL
1 teaspoon = 5 mL
1 tablespoon = 15 mL
2 tablespoons = 30 mL
$1/4$ cup = 60 mL
$1/3$ cup = 75 mL
$1/2$ cup = 125 mL
$2/3$ cup = 150 mL
$3/4$ cup = 175 mL
1 cup = 250 mL
2 cups = 1 pint = 500 mL
3 cups = 750 mL
4 cups = 1 quart = 1 L

VOLUME MEASUREMENTS (fluid)

1 fluid ounce (2 tablespoons) = 30 mL
4 fluid ounces ($1/2$ cup) = 125 mL
8 fluid ounces (1 cup) = 250 mL
12 fluid ounces ($1 1/2$ cups) = 375 mL
16 fluid ounces (2 cups) = 500 mL

WEIGHTS (mass)

$1/2$ ounce = 15 g
1 ounce = 30 g
3 ounces = 90 g
4 ounces = 120 g
8 ounces = 225 g
10 ounces = 285 g
12 ounces = 360 g
16 ounces = 1 pound = 450 g

DIMENSIONS

$1/16$ inch = 2 mm
$1/8$ inch = 3 mm
$1/4$ inch = 6 mm
$1/2$ inch = 1.5 cm
$3/4$ inch = 2 cm
1 inch = 2.5 cm

OVEN TEMPERATURES

250°F = 120°C
275°F = 140°C
300°F = 150°C
325°F = 160°C
350°F = 180°C
375°F = 190°C
400°F = 200°C
425°F = 220°C
450°F = 230°C

BAKING PAN SIZES

Utensil	Size in Inches/Quarts	Metric Volume	Size in Centimeters
Baking or Cake Pan (square or rectangular)	$8 \times 8 \times 2$	2 L	$20 \times 20 \times 5$
	$9 \times 9 \times 2$	2.5 L	$23 \times 23 \times 5$
	$12 \times 8 \times 2$	3 L	$30 \times 20 \times 5$
	$13 \times 9 \times 2$	3.5 L	$33 \times 23 \times 5$
Loaf Pan	$8 \times 4 \times 3$	1.5 L	$20 \times 10 \times 7$
	$9 \times 5 \times 3$	2 L	$23 \times 13 \times 7$
Round Layer Cake Pan	$8 \times 1 1/2$	1.2 L	20×4
	$9 \times 1 1/2$	1.5 L	23×4
Pie Plate	$8 \times 1 1/4$	750 mL	20×3
	$9 \times 1 1/4$	1 L	23×3
Baking Dish or Casserole	1 quart	1 L	—
	$1 1/2$ quart	1.5 L	—
	2 quart	2 L	—